# Admiral Seymour's Expedition & TAKU FORTS 1900

Colin Narbeth

Copyright 1980 Colin Narbeth
First published by Picton Publishing 1980
ISBN 0 902633 69 4

All rights reserved.
No part of this publication may be reproduced, stored
in a retrieval system, or transmitted, in any form or by any means, electronic,
mechanical, photocopying, recording or otherwise, without the prior
permission of the copyright owners.

Phototypeset in 9/11 pt Plantin
by Chippenham Typesetting, Bath Road, Chippenham, Wiltshire.
Text paper supplied by Howard Smith Papers, Bristol.
Bound by Western Book Co. Ltd. Maesteg Glamorgan.
Printed in Great Britain by Picton Print
Citadel Works, Bath Road, Chippenham, Wiltshire
PP30247

# PRELUDE

The China campaign of 1900 – war was never declared, came about through a people's uprising under the banner of the Society of Boxers, whose avowed intention was to expel foreigners from China. The ruling authority first opposed, then tolerated and finally supported the Boxers. The unruly and ruffian elements of China's youth rushed to the movement and came to believe, through the teachings of their elders, that they had invincibility against the foreigners. That if they were killed they would rise again.

Against this rabble the European powers took the very minimal precaution of sending about 400 men to guard their Legations in Peking. The spears, bows and arrows, and odd assortment of guns, some of which were more dangerous to the users than to their enemies, presented little problem. The undoubted, dedicated courage of the Boxers was to cause some alarm. Then, when further Allied forces were sent to strengthen the Legations, the sudden confrontation by Imperial Chinese troops, caught the Allies on the wrong foot. A state of war existed even if it was not declared, and now the Chinese were using modern rifles and Krupps quick-firing guns which the Germans had, to their regret, provided and trained them with.

Yet it was Germany more than other nations who did most to ferment the Boxer movement. After the Sino-Japanese War had exposed the weakness of China, the powerful nations of the world descended on her like vultures to carve up the spoils. In diplomatic language it was merely 'spheres of influence', in practice it meant an armed presence. When two missionaries were butchered by fanatical Boxers, Germany seized the occasion to take Kiaochow Bay and Tsingtao as reprisals. This, more than subsequent actions of a similar nature, enraged the Chinese.

By May 1900 the Boxers erupted. An international fleet gathered off Taku ready to protect their nationals and the Legation Guard took up their duties. While ambassadors were indicating that the troubles seemed to be evaporating, they suddenly got worse. Telegraph lines were cut, railway lines demolished, and Peking was cut off. Vice-Admiral Seymour promptly landed with an international force of 2,000 men and set off to relieve Peking. He was stopped in his tracks by Imperial Chinese troops. At the same time Tientsin, the halfway house between Peking and Taku, was put under siege. All communication with Seymour ceased and the foreign powers were fighting for survival in both Peking and Tientsin.

Taku took on an ominous importance. Who now controlled Taku, controlled the outcome. Unless the Allies could take Taku they would have no firm base from which to operate and to succour the Legations. The battle of the Taku Forts was the most important of the campaign.

# THE SEYMOUR EXPEDITION

The Boxer Movement spread like wildfire from its birthplace, Shantung. For a long time the European powers saw no danger in the movement. Untrained peasantry, they could be put down at any time – a modern counterpart would be skinheads on a day out at Brighton; but suddenly joined by the police! Catastrophe.

Staff Paymaster F. C. Alton Secretary     Flag-Lieutenant F. A. Powlett     Flag-Captain J. R. Jellicoe
Vice-Admiral Sir Edward Hobart Seymour, K.C.B., and Staff.

Vice-Admiral Sir Edward Hobart Seymour, K.C.B, Commander-in-Chief, China Station, who flew his flag in HMS *Centurion*, remained calm as the temperature grew. But he was sufficiently worried to make a personal trip on June 3 to study the position for himself. He also prepared more guards for the Legations – but was told they were not needed. When the British Consul at Tientsin asked that men should be able 'to take active measures of hostility', he denied such authority. He reported to the Admiralty, '. . . I heard that an attack had been made a day or two previously on an armed party of over thirty Belgians who were coming in with their families from Pao-ting-fu, on the Peking-Hankau railway line now under construction. It was supposed that some of the party had been killed as nine were missing.

I was also informed of the murder of an English missionary, Mr Robinson, and the abduction of another, Mr Norman, at Yungching, some thirty miles from Tientsin. Bishop Scott asked me to send out a party to attempt to rescue Mr Norman, but before any action could be taken it was ascertained that he too had been murdered.'

The Boxers were to kill some 250 missionaries during the uprising. The most notable massacre of Christians being at Taiyuan on July 9 when the Governor, Yu Hsien, supervised the execution of forty-five people including women and children. When the white-bearded Roman Catholic Bishop attempted to remonstrate the Governor drew his ceremonial sword and silenced him with one slash across the face. Yu Hsien was subsequently executed at the insistence of the foreign powers.

Hatred of the foreign missionaries was the natural result of treaties obtained by force of arms which required that missionaries could reside and preach in inland cities and were to have 'mandarin' status. As one modern observer put it – it was rather like the British Government suddenly announcing that henceforth witchdoctors were to be on a par with National Health doctors. The majority of the 'converts' were 'rice-christians' – they went along for the rice rations. Although not fanatically religious the Chinese had highly-developed religions, like Buddhism; and community life was based on a set of values derived from the teachings of Confucius. Villagers contributed to the cost of religious celebrations – and when Christian converts opted out it meant the other villagers had to pay more. Naturally they grew to dislike the Christians.

When on June 9, at the third emergency conference of senior officers, Admiral Seymour read a telegram from H.M. Minister stating that unless those in Peking were relieved soon it would be too late, he ended by saying that he would start out at once with all available men. The time was 1.30pm. His rider, that he hoped the Allies would co-operate, did not detract from the clear intention to go it alone if necessary. Whether he would have plunged into such a venture had he known the true position is open to some doubt. He thought he was facing a large but unruly mob of Boxers. He did not expect to meet Imperial troops – indeed he expected them to be on his side!

He wrote to the Admiralty: 'The situation at the Palace was said to be strained, the Dowager Empress being credited with a wish to put down the Boxers, but not daring to do so on account of their numbers and support by some of the princes . . .'

Admiral Seymour had received intelligence that General Nieh had been ordered by the Chinese Government to suppress the rebels assembling in large numbers near Tientsin, and had killed five hundred of them in a sharp engagement. He recorded: 'It appears from subsequent information that this number was greatly exaggerated'.

There were three routes to Peking open to him. By railway the distance was 85 miles; by road 75 miles; by river to Tung-Chow 55 miles (plus the last 20 miles by road).

General Nieh

Normally the train journey would take just three hours. The line from Tientsin curved erratically with the Pei-ho as far as Yangtsun. There the line crossed the river and went parallel to Hun-ho skirting the Imperial hunting grounds, to Feng-tai and there branching off to Machia-po, the end of the line a mile and a half from the southern wall of Peking.

By road the journey would take at least two days; the road being a badly rutted cart-track. The river route would take five days and was only advisable in the rainy season when the roads were impassable. Admiral Seymour decided to go by train.

*June 10* At 9.30am the relief force began to move out of Tientsin by train. The speed of the operation can be gauged by the fact that the men had been landed the previous night in the destroyers *Fame* and *Whiting*, and a tug, and had reached Tientsin at 7.30am. Admiral Seymour wasted little time. His train had onboard 300 British seamen and marines, 112 Americans, forty Italians, and twenty-five Austrians. The fierce sun had long since bleached the green from what foliage there was and a blanket of airless heat engulfed the men of the naval brigade. It was exclusively a naval brigade though three civilians accompanied them. Mr Clive Bigham, honorary attaché to the Peking Legation, as intelligence officer; Mr Archibald Currie, C.B. of the Peking-Tientsin railway, as engineer and Mr C. W. Campbell, British consul for Wuchow.

Whatever spare room there was had been filled with sleepers and materials for repairing the rail-lines ahead. For 36 miles they made good progress. Just beyond Yangtsun the position became extremely tense. Rifle bolts were cocked and every man was alert. The train chugged its way by the camp of General Nieh who had some 4,000 Imperial troops at his command. The soldiers showed neither fear nor hostility, but a curiosity shared by the men in the train. Nevertheless, one word from either commander and the whole area would have burst into violence. The danger was soon over and for another ten miles the train chugged its way over the flat, dull land covered with its eerie mounds of kraal-shaped Chinese graves which seemed to stretch endlessly to the horizon.

Near Lofa Station the train came to a stop because of damage to the line. It was 3.30pm and the repair work started. There was plenty of muscle and skill and the officers had allowed for repair work to take up to two days. But after a few hours of plate-laying and shovelling at the burned up ground the pace of work noticeably slackened. Water was put on ration. The

Chinese Army at drill on the racecourse, Peking.

Boxers had done their job better than the Allies expected. Huge fires had been lit under the bridges which tended to warp the rails as well as destroying the wooden sleepers. Admiral Seymour decided to camp where he was for the night and in the evening two more trains filled with bluejackets and marines joined him.

Railway bridge on the Peking Line, stripped of rails.
In the distance a Chinese barricade and gun.

*June 11* Early in the morning the three trains proceeded to Lofa Station where the engines were watered. A fourth train joined up with them at the station with 200 Russians and fifty-eight French, making a total force at Seymour's command of over 2,000. The force left Lofa at 11.30am leaving behind a guard of one officer, Lieutenant Horatio Walcott Colomb, and thirty men (later to be reinforced to sixty men).

At 6.00pm the Allied force had its first brush with the Boxers. The force was some three miles from Langfang Station. Seymour's laconic report read: 'Some Boxers were seen approaching; they had previously endeavoured to cut off an advanced party with railway repairing gear, but had failed, and now came to the attack of No. 1 train (commanded by Capt. McCalla, U.S.N.); they advanced in skirmishing order, and were soon repulsed by our rifle fire, leaving about thirty-five killed.'

But a somewhat more detailed account has been left for posterity by one of the men of the Naval Brigade who wrote: 'A huge mob of Chinese nearly cut off a small party of marines reconnoitring on a trolley ahead, and then tried to rush the train. Of course, companies immediately went out on both flanks, so there was no firing from the front truck, as our own men were in the woods all round us. The enemy got within about a hundred yards of us. You probably know all about them wearing red stuff, and thinking themselves invulnerable. Most of them are armed with swords or spears, and only a few have antiquated rifles. I suppose they are very like Dervishes before they attack. They kow-tow, and then come on in a rush. Their great trick is shamming dead and then getting up behind you. One of our young midshipmen had a very narrow shave with a man armed with a sword (blade 5 feet and handle $4\frac{1}{2}$ feet long), but he luckily hit him in the hands first shot. They retired very soon, although their main body, with some cavalry, never came into action. We had no casualties, but the Admiral was very near it, as he went up into the firing line without any arms, with the secretary, and got separated, and a man rose up between them, but very luckily the secretary shot him, otherwise it would have been a certainty. I think we killed forty or fifty; some of them boys . . . till we got to Langfang where the water was good; and that was the first I'd had, as we had been awfully short of water before.'

Clive Bigham also left an account of the action: 'Not more than a couple of hundred, armed with swords, spears, gingals and rifles, many of them being quite boys. To anyone who has been some little time in China it was an almost incredible sight, for there was no sign of fear or hesitation, and these were not fanatical "braves" or the trained soldiers of the Empress, but quiet, peaceloving peasantry – the countryside in arms against the foreigner.'

One of the problems facing the Allies was the belief among Boxers that they were 'invulnerable' to the foreigners' bullets. Bigham, in particular, was astounded at his own inablility to convince a Chinese servant that this was not so. Looking at the dead Boxers the servant merely remarked that they were not true Boxers 'only make-believe'. Others maintained that in a few days the dead would rise up to fight again. The British, because of this, deliberately left the dead to rot in the open.

The problem of Chinese feigning death was quickly overcome. In future all Boxers were put to death on the spot unless wanted for interrogation. A few of the prisoners taken at this first encounter were sent back to Tientsin by train arriving on June 13. David Beatty commented: 'a train arrived with the news that the Pekin Relief Column had been attacked by Boxers, of whom they had killed and wounded a large number, a few of the latter being sent down in the train and proving to be mostly youths of irresponsible age.'

*June 12* It now became apparent that the Chinese had systematically destroyed the railway lines. The men were not endeared to the Chinese now that they had to bend their backs in the burning sun to repair the damage. They made four miles in the day. The two days' provisions – ample one might have thought to cover any emergency that a few hours' train journey could bring – was gone. Nearby villages were burned to the ground. Because the expedition was ill-prepared for a sustained campaign they were soon having to loot the buildings and among the most prized items were kettles and bowls for boiling water. Pigs and chickens, deserted in the Chinese villages at the approach of the naval brigade, were soon in the cooking pot.

At Langfang it was clear that the lines ahead were badly damaged and, as some of the sleepers were still smouldering, that the damage was fresh. Seymour decided to rest his men. In order to stop the Boxers doing any more damage he ordered Lieutenant Arthur Gordon Smith, Gunnery Officer of the *Aurora* to take three officers and forty-four men of *Aurora* to Anting Station, 13 miles ahead where he was to hold the station and prevent damage to the lines.

Torn up rails. Notice the stone rifle pits at the side.

The Allies, even at this stage, saw no reason for alarm and many of the British seamen spent the time decorating the engines of the trains with captured Boxer standards.

*June 13* Lieutenant Smith and his men took post in a native village at Anting early in the morning. Admiral Seymour reported to the Admiralty: '. . . and early in that morning was attacked by Boxers three times in succession, who, however, retreated on a few volleys being fired, with a loss of fifteen men. At 10.30am a final and more determined attack was made by about 450 Boxers, who charged in line with great courage and enthusiasm, but were repulsed with heavy loss, estimated (with those killed in previous attacks) to be about 150.'

Lieutenant Smith had marched out the previous day, each man with a hundred rounds and one day's water and food. He had fortified a joss-house but it now became clear the position was untenable. The patrol abandoned the remaining provisions and fought a hasty retreat – remarkable in that no casualties were suffered.

Seymour attached great importance to the possession of Anting in order to allow the railway to be repaired for the continued advance to Peking. So he now sent out an even stronger force, under Major Johnstone R.M.L.I. of sixty marines. Major Johnstone advanced a few miles but was then attacked at a spot where a full mile of the line had been ripped up and destroyed. He drove off the Boxers killing some twenty-five of them and then decided to retire on Langfang as the destruction he had been sent out to prevent had already been achieved by the Boxers. He was to arrive back at Langfang on the evening of the 14th when Admiral Seymour, somewhat oddly one might think, was sending his last despatch to Sir Claude MacDonald, 'Am confident of entering city. Hope in a few days.'

*June 14* Up until June 14 the foreign powers had suffered no casualties, nor had they any real difficulty in dispersing Boxers. Only advance patrols had been obliged to retreat. But now the Boxers carried the fight to the Allies and came in force at Langfang.

A force of 2,000 crept up to the lines and made a sudden attack gaining complete surprise – many of the British being stripped to the waist and 'watering at the well'. Most surprised was the Italian picket, and the first the Allies knew of the attack was when they heard the fearful cries of the five Italians as they were hacked to pieces. They had been caught fair and square playing cards. Seymour's choice of the word 'deplore' in his official report thus may have been intended to have two meanings. He wrote:

Italians standing by the train. Five of them got caught napping at cards by the Chinese while on picket duty. They were all killed.

'At about 10.15am the outposts were seen running in and reported the Boxers close to in great numbers; they were closely followed by the Boxers, who made a most determined rush at the fore part of the train which was then drawn up alongside a well, where many of our men were engaged in watering. They came on in great numbers in loose formation and with the utmost courage under a withering fire, some of them even reaching the train before they were killed. They did not retreat until they had suffered a loss of about one hundred. I regret to say that we have to deplore the loss of five Italians, who formed the picket near a deserted village, which was used by the Boxers to conceal their approach.'

Other sources indicate that it was a bit more hectic than the Admiral's report would suggest with one man writing: 'Nearly all hands were in the village bathing and carrying water, and till we began to arrive it was a pretty close thing, lots arriving fresh from the bath, having left their clothes. The chaplain and a doctor had to defend the "wardroom" for a bit, and several other people got their swords home.' Some of the Chinese reached the lead train and were bayoneted from the top of the tender. The naval officer who formed the firing line in front of the lead train set up a Maxim gun with the casualness of parade ground training while howls of *Towah! Towah!* (Kill! Kill!) echoed all round him from fanatical Chinese. He wrote: 'It seemed awfully unreal . . . this mowing down of men but a few yards off'. Maxim bullets were heavy large lead bullets rather like the outlawed dum-dums of the Great War. It was soon found that fanatical Chinese were capable of carrying on the momentum of their charge even after they should, by all medical accounts, have been dead against the nickel-jacketed rifle bullets. The Maxim bullets however, crushed them like a pile driver.

Admiral Seymour was now beginning to get apprehensive. No communication had been possible with his base since the 13th. The men watched as a trolley hurtled down the line towards them that evening. It was a messenger (he arrived at 5.30pm) with the news that the small guard left at Lofa was under heavy attack. It was sinister intelligence. His rear as well as his front was threatened. The Admiral took command of train No.2 himself and raced back to Lofa. There he found that the little garrison under Lieutenant Colomb had fortified a house which they had named 'Fort Endymion' after their ship. Several thousand Chinese had attacked and for the first time had used artillery. Fortunately for the guard they were two medieval guns from which they literally fired railway nuts and bolts as well as stones. Among the wounded, one of *Endymion's* men was badly hit by a stone fired this way which struck his right lung. He later died. The guard beat off the attack and killed around a hundred Chinese. The reinforcements under Seymour harassed the retreating Chinese.

*June 15* Although Admiral Seymour had still not given up the idea of relieving Peking he now decided on a change of plan. 'It appeared to me probable that the attempt to relieve Peking might have to be made by river . . .' Food, water and ammunition were short. One sailor wrote: 'I don't know how we should have lived without looting, as we left the ship in such a hurry that we brought practically nothing with us. Of course we get our rations, but "Fanny Adams" (slang: preserved meat) and biscuit began to pall after a little. The worst part has been want of water. We have been so hard up as to drink tea made with the engine's exhaust.'

The Allies were obliged to stay at Langfang during the 15th. A working party set about repairing the line ahead with a strong guard detached with the construction train to protect the workers. A train which had been sent back to Lofa returned and reported that the line which had been repaired had been broken up again. Later on the officer of the station guard at Lofa came up with an engine and reported that he thought an attack in force by Boxers might be expected, as he had seen three large bodies moving about in the distance. They eventually moved off without attacking. They were probably content with destroying the lines further along.

*June 16* An effort was now made early in the morning to send a train back to Tientsin. The train returned at 3.00pm with the news that the railway was so badly damaged between Lofa and Yangtsun as to be beyond repair with the resources carried by the Allies. Admiral Seymour took train No.1 and went back to investigate for himself. (The previous day in fact, Captain Burke had tried to get a train through from Tientsin to Lofa with supplies but had also found the line impassable.) Nos.2 and 3 trains (manned by *Endymion* and *Aurora*) stayed at Langfang and No.4, which contained no British or Americans was at Lofa. Every effort was now exerted to renew communications with Yangtsun and this meant eight miles of slogging repair work in the unyielding heat. But the men realised the necessity for success and the line to Yangtsun was open by evening. There the Admiral found the bridge impassable and the line destroyed as far as he could see.

German Marines

The Germans dug in at Langfang fortifying a position near the station which they named 'Fort Gefion'. Stores were fast running out and the order was given to go on field rations. Enterprising sailors were able to give variety to their diet with the local chickens and black pigs – these quite common little beasts were later to return the compliment, feeding on the corpses which scattered the battlefields.

Seymour's plan was to fall back on Yangtsun and from there go by boat – the route followed by Anglo-French forces in 1860.

*June 17* Orders went out recalling trains 2, 3 and 4 from Lofa and Langfang. All were to concentrate on Yangtsun. Admiral Seymour wrote: 'A few days previously I had endeavoured to send down orders to Tientsin for junks, provisions and ammunition to be sent to Yangtsun with a view to establishing a base there from which to start, if found desirable, by river to Tungchow, marching thence to Peking, as our alternative route. Not one of these couriers reached Tientsin, the surrounding country being at that time overrun with Boxers or hostile Chinese. I had also tried to get messages to the General at Hong Kong.'

He now acknowledged the possibility of the isolation and separate destruction of the trains. His forces were too spread out. Admiral Seymour was set on bringing them all together. Another disturbing factor was that he could hear artillery fire from the direction of Tientsin. He had no knowledge of events in Tientsin.

*June 18* This was a black day for the expedition and resulted in the decision to give up the attempt to relieve Peking. Admiral Seymour recorded the events: 'No.3 returned on the afternoon of the 18th, and in the evening Nos.2 and 4 from Langfang. Captain von Usedom of His Imperial German Majesty's Navy, the senior officer present with Nos.2 and 4 trains, reported that they had had a severe engagement with the enemy, who unexpectedly attacked them at Langfang about 2.30pm on that day in great force estimated to be fully 5,000 men including cavalry, large numbers of whom were armed with magazine rifles of the latest pattern. The banners captured show them to have belonged to the army of General Tung Fu Hsiang (an ex-bandit whose Kansu fighters were favoured by the Empress), who commands the Chinese troops in the Hunting Park outside Peking, and it was thus definitely known for the first time that Imperial Chinese troops were being employed against us!'

The attack had commenced against 'Fort Gefion' and encouraged by numerical superiority the Chinese began to press home. British and French seamen were hastily moved up to help the German contingent. The battle closed to hand-to-hand fighting and when the Imperial troops finally retired after two very determined attacks, they left 400 dead on the field. Six Allied men were killed and forty-eight wounded. The Germans captured four junks which were to prove very useful in the next few days.

*June 19* Admiral Seymour convened a meeting of the heads of the naval force and it did not take them long to unanimously agree to retreat to Tientsin. The position was untenable. They had few provisions, were short of ammunition and were now engaging the Imperial Army of China, as well as enormous hoards of Boxers. The wounded were loaded into the captured junks, the trains abandoned and at 3.00pm the withdrawal started. A long delay was caused by the junks grounding in the shallow reach of the river, and one could not be floated off until a six-pounder quick firing gun from *Centurion* was thrown overboard. The force made $2\frac{1}{2}$ miles down the river and then bivouacked for the night without further incident. The officers had buried their full-dress uniforms. Only essential equipment was to be carried now. All could hear the Chinese celebrating and could see the glow as their trains were burned to cinders. Nor were they to be left to retreat on Tientsin – and they now knew that Tientsin was being fired on by the Chinese!

*June 20* At 9.15am the Chinese attacked. The able-bodied men were in heavy marching order and on half rations which would run out in two days. The night had given them little rest; they had learned that worse than the heat were the damp mists which came up from the mosquito-infested banks and saturated the tired men. The wounded suffered interminably. Several villages in succession had to be carried either by rifle fire, or failing that, at the point of the bayonet. 'The charge with bayonets,' wrote Admiral Seymour,' was always very effective, the cheers of the men as they advanced appearing to intimidate the Chinese, who without waiting to receive the charge would fall back immediately.'

In the afternoon the Chinese brought into action a one-pounder quick firing gun and although not much damage was done by it the effect of its fire was nerve-racking to men exposed on the march in open spaces. The Chinese used smokeless powder to mask the gun's position. Eight miles were made during the day. Every village that had to be attacked was burned to the ground without mercy despite the protestations of the old men and women who knelt beside their burning homes wringing their hands and wailing. A one-pounder Hotchkiss was captured after retreating Chinese tried to hide it in a swamp at the rear of a village. For a time the Allies were concerned at the ferocity of Chinese fire. Then it was discovered that they were using an old trick – the 'cracker guns'. A bayonet charge had succeeded in dislodging the Chinese and burned crackers were found in abundance. At the next village the charge was made a bit more buoyantly! (This old Chinese trick of gun-crackers was used as late as World War II when on D-Day such crackers were dropped by parachute to confuse defenders.)

*June 21* The march was resumed at 7.30am. Then a force of cavalry was seen on the horizon. Judging from the formation Seymour took them to be Russian Cossacks. The Russian colours were hoisted by a delighted force – but in answer came a well directed Chinese shell. Admiral Seymour was about to be engaged by General Nieh's army, 8,000-strong and with four batteries.

The fighting was fierce and continuous, allowing Seymour to make only six miles in a fighting retreat. Admiral Seymour wrote: 'A few minutes after the withdrawal of the cavalry the enemy opened fire with a field gun and one-pounder quick firing. Their fire was returned by our nine-pounder and machine guns, and the position of their field gun being disclosed by its smoke our fire was successful in checking it; although it was brought into action again during the day from time to time, but with the same result as soon as its position was known.

Fighting was carried on continuously throughout a succession of villages and in the town of Peitsang, which is the chief place between Tientsin and Yangtsun, and at 6.00pm, the enemy being then in a very strong position from which we were unable to dislodge them during the evening, a halt was made.'

Russian Marines

The Germans, Russians and Japanese were on the right-hand side of the river and the rest of the force on the left. The British cleared the first village and occupied it but the second village was heavily defended. British and Americans charged against well directed fire, their own artillery being unable to help as it was heavily engaged by General Nieh's artillery. In the brief rush many casualties occurred including Admiral Seymour's chief-of-staff, Captain Jellicoe (at first his wound was thought to be mortal). The Allies were checked and took cover by some banks, rallied and charged again. This time the Chinese fled. No time was given to the Chinese to fall back on the third village and defend it. The British carried the charge straight to it and routed the Chinese.

A positional battle developed along European lines with the Allied line of British, Americans and French all advancing with one flank resting on the sand-bank – the Chinese moving to the other end of the sand-bank and from its crest making a stand. Captain McCalla of the U.S. Navy led two companies of *Centurion*'s men and thirty Americans to attack and turn the enemy flank. The operation was a complete success but the exhilerated force carried on the advance to the fourth village where they were suddenly confronted by a strong garrison of Imperial troops. At the same time heavy fire broke out from across the river as well-entrenched Chinese joined battle in support of their comrades, they themselves not yet being attacked by the Russians and Germans. The little force under McCalla had to retreat with further loss of officers and men. Captain McCalla was himself wounded. (In fact he was wounded on three separate occasions during the expedition).

*June 22* Admiral Seymour decided that the situation was getting very serious. He halted and gave his men five hours rest before at 1.00am the 'Fall In' was sounded. He hoped to snake his column past the Chinese in the dark. It was not to be. The Chinese were not caught napping and signal fires burst out. The field and machine guns had been placed in a junk and there was now little room for the wounded who had doubled from the previous day's fighting. Two hundred yards from a village the Chinese opened a galling fire. The force had managed one and a half miles. The junk carrying the guns was struck by Chinese shells and sunk. Only the Maxims were saved. The marines fixed bayonets and carried the position.

At 4.00am the column became aware of a black mass looming up ahead of them in the darkness. It was the enormous Hsiku Arsenal – whose existence was totally unknown to the Allies. Two unarmed Chinese soldiers came out to ask who the foreigners were and what they wanted. It all seemed unreal. The interpreter explained that the force was friendly to the Chinese Government and wished to be allowed to pass peaceably to Tientsin. The Chinese seemed friendly enough and walked back to the building they had come from. The moment they were inside the Chinese opened up with everything they had from every direction possible. Only the darkness saved the head of the column from total annihiliation. Fortunately good cover was at hand in a village and behind the river embankment. The rear columns had not yet come up nor the wounded in the junks. But one junk full of wounded broke loose and careered over to the Chinese side of the river. Captain McCalla, U.S.N. recorded the incident: 'Among the many acts of courage during the day was a deed of conspicuous bravery and readiness of resource which reflects credit upon the whole naval profession and was done by one British bluejacket from the *Centurion*, Edward Turner, and Seaman George, from the *Aurora*. (In fact McCalla got it wrong, George really belonged to *Orlando*). Shortly after the enemy opened fire from the arsenal grounds, one of the junks in which there were British and American wounded drifted across the river, and grounded against the bank occupied by the Chinese. These two bluejackets, forming a part of the guard of the junk, sprang overboard, and, pushing the junk afloat, towed her out of the line of fire, and anchored her securely to the bank.'

A number of the wounded were killed during the time it took to reach safety; but had not the two seamen taken swift action it was likely the whole lot would have been killed. Gold medals from the Life Saving Association of New York, with personal letters of thanks from the Secretary of the U.S. Navy, were subsequently forwarded to both men. George also received the Conspicuous Gallantry Medal.

Admiral Seymour attacked at once. His report states: 'Rifle fire was directed to a 47mm Hotchkiss gun at the north corner of the Armoury, and two 10cm guns on the river front. Some of the men at the guns were killed and others driven from them.

Major Johnstone, R.M.L.I. of the *Centurion*, was then sent higher up the river to cross over unobserved, with a party of a hundred marines and seamen, to rush the position at the north corner. There is a village about 150 yards from this, which enabled the attacking force to come up without being seen until they emerged from it, when they charged with a cheer, joined in by those on the other side of the river; and the Chinese in that part of the Armoury fled precipitately. At the same time, lower down the river, a German detachment crossed over and captured two guns (10cm Krupp) in their front, and subsequently several others. The two detachments then cleared the whole Armoury grounds.'

But it was fierce fighting and lasted an hour, the British barely able to hold their own, possessing neither the numbers nor the local knowledge of the enemy, who were able to harrass them considerably from buildings and other positions which the Allies did not understand how to get at because of the complicated arrangement of the houses and moats. It did not take them long, however, to turn the enemy's guns onto the nearby village where most of the Chinese had fled. The Chinese infantry tried to retake the Armoury before the main force could come up but the little garrison held them off and caused severe losses. But Commander Buchholtz of the German Navy was among the killed during that defence.

It was some time before the Allies realised the extent of their victory. The Arsenal was enormous being a mile in circumference. The Arsenal was full, one observer estimated the value of the ammunition, weapons and food to be in the region of three million pounds. At any rate the men came off half-rations at once! That evening Seymour sent out a party of one hundred marines under Captains Doig and Lloyd, with Mr Currie as guide, to try and reach Tientsin. But the force was immediately attacked and it was soon clear that it was going to be defeated unless it retreated back to the Arsenal, which it did. Admiral Seymour realised that his best bet was to sit tight. He had enough ammunition and food to hold out almost indefinitely.

That night the charger of one of the Chinese officers who had fallen while charging the Armoury, was cooked and eaten.

*June 23* General Nieh launched a counter-attack soon after dawn with an estimated twenty-five battalions. The attacks went on until 8.00am and caused a number of Allied casualties including the death of Captain Herbert William Hope Beyts, R.M.A. of *Centurion*. (He had been company officer of *Centurion*'s marines and those duties were then taken over by Engineer George Herbert Cockey.) The Allies had time to take stock. They found fifteen tons of rice, supplies of medical equipment, bandages (the Allies were right out of bandages and had been using the pugarees from officers' and marines helmets). There were seven million rounds of ammunition. The Russians and Japanese were out of ammunition and were re-armed with Mausers from the Armoury. There was Lee-Metford ammunition enough to last the British force for months. The Allied wounded now numbered 232. This prevented any attempt to reach Tientsin in force.

Japanese cremating their own dead after battle.

But Admiral Seymour determined to make contact and more couriers were sent. The Admiral also turned the guns of the Arsenal on to a Chinese fort further down the river which seemed to have excellent effect.

*June 24* Although none of the couriers had got through so far, this day Bigham's Chinese servant successfully reached Tientsin. He was caught by Boxers and tied to a tree. He had eaten his message and was eventually freed. Then Imperial troops questioned him and finally a French outpost threatened his life. But he managed to arrive at the British Consulate with the latest news.

Vicious sandstorms for most of the day quietened the Chinese attacks. A Chinese soldier, wounded and captured while trying to enter the Armoury stated that General Nieh's army were much discouraged at their want of success, and that the attempts to retake the Armoury were made with twenty-five battalions (nominally of 500 men each, but probably of not more than 300 to 400 men). The storms did not prevent the Allies from continuing to bombard the Chinese with their own guns.

The defence was re-arranged with the British and Germans sharing the three most dangerous walls, the Americans and Russians the fourth wall while the French and Japanese did the sentry and picket duties, and defended the inner line. Tents were discovered and were quickly pitched to afford some protection from the sandstorms which penetrated nearly everything. At first the Chinese used long range fire but after 10.00am they attacked the north front in force causing several casualties. When they were beaten off they resorted to sniper tactics. Picked marksmen were chosen from the Allied force to mark them man for man while the rest of the men were able to rest.

*June 25* Early in the morning one of the guns in the fort below the Armoury was observed to be firing towards Tientsin. Admiral Seymour ordered two guns to be put into position to bombard it and create a diversion. The Chinese gun then turned its fire towards the Armoury. Sharp rifle fire was heard and the Chinese cavalry were seen to retire. A little later Cossack cavalry came into sight under the Russian Colonel Shirinski. Soon the Seymour Expedition was relieved.

Return of Admiral Seymours Naval Brigade.

Arrangements had been made by Captain Bayly with the Russian General for the despatch of a force to relieve the Peking Expeditionary Force after Bigham's messenger had got through. The Russian General provided 1,000 men with two guns, and 900 men were furnished by the remainder of the garrison at Tientsin (600 being British) with two Maxims. They had started out at midnight.

Com. D. Beatty HMS *Barfleur*

David Beatty accompanied the expedition to relieve Seymour and wrote: 'We started with a force of 500 seamen under myself, 180 marines under Luke, 150 Welsh Regiment, 100 Americans, 70 Italians, all under Captain Cradock, to go to the Russian Camp. After losing our way in that short distance we eventually arrived and started off again with 900 Russians and 100 Germans making altogether 2,000 men under my old friend Colonel Shirinski. We followed the Great Wall, which traversed the surrounding country and completely gave us cover from the forts, and although owing to the want of guides mistook our way, eventually arrived at the river, here we became exposed for the first time to the shell-fire from the forts. The horses had all to be swum across, and the men scrambled over the broken-down bridge, but after we were once over, we had no further difficulties . . . We sighted the White Ensign flying amongst some trees on the river and arrived.'

The Hsiku Arsenal was subsequently destroyed.

# OFFICERS MENTIONED IN DESPATCHES

'Captain John R. Jellicoe, my Flag Captain, who was, as always, of most valuable help, both by his judgement and action, till disabled by a serious wound at the battle of Peitsang on 21st June.

Commander Charles D. Graville, of my Flagship, who ably commanded the Naval Brigade with me after my Flag Captain was wounded.

Commander William O. Boothby, of HMS *Endymion*, in command of the seamen from that ship, and at times, of others also. He was in every engagement, and I specially noticed his energy and activity.

Lieutenant George M. K. Fair, of my Flagship, employed on my Staff in Intelligence Department, etc., but diverted as required to other duties, such as the very important one of getting along the junks with wounded.

Lieutenant Horatio W. Colomb, of HMS *Endymion*, was twice slightly wounded on different days. He had charge of Lofa Station Fort, defended it against various attacks, and showed good judgement while in separate command.

Lieutenant Edward G. Lowther-Crofton, of my Flagship, most intelligent and active; with great risk to himself he remained behind in the Hsiku Armoury on 26th instant, when we left for Tientsin, to set fire to and destroy it, having made the preparations for so doing, which were carried out by him most satisfactorily. This important service reflects very great credit on him.

Lieutenant Arthur G. Smith, of HMS *Aurora*, led and commanded an advanced post above Langfang, on the line towards Peking, with zeal and good judgement.

Midshipman William B. C. Jones of HMS *Centurion* who took command of Lieutenant Wyndham L. Bamber's company in the operations on 21st June, after the latter officer was wounded.

Mr Charles Davidge, Acting Gunner of *Centurion*, who ably assisted Lieutenant Crofton in the destruction of Hsiku Armoury, and shared the risks with him – they two being alone.

Major James R. Johnstone, R.M.L.I. of *Centurion* has been most active throughout. He often commanded all the marines present. He kept pushing ahead of the trains on our advance, to clear and protect the line. He it was who led the storming party I sent round on 22nd June to carry the north angle of the Armoury, near Hsiku, and he has rendered very good service.

Captain Richard O. M. Doig, R.M.L.I., HMS *Endymion*, has been very active throughout and commanded the night expedition of one hundred men, on 22nd June, sent from the Armoury to try and communication with Tientsin, which attempt he made with skill and credit.

Mr Francis C. Alton, my secretary, has been near me throughout, and, as at all times, was of the greatest assistance and value by his grasp of matters and good judgement and sense.

Mr Charles J. E. Rotter, assistant paymaster of my Flagship, was in charge of the commissariat arrangements, a most difficult task under the circumstances, but performed by him with constant efforts and all possible success. To this, having regard to our foreign allies, Mr Rotter's knowledge of German, and well known tact and good temper, much contributed.

Fleet Surgeon Thomas M. Sibbald, HMS *Centurion*, has had charge of the hospital arrangements throughout, and has also been much under fire. His activity, attention, and constant cheerfulness have gone far to mitigate the sufferings of the wounded, and have met with my entire approval.

Mr George H. Cockey, Engineer, HMS *Centurion*, took over the duties of company officer of the *Centurion*'s marine detachment after Captain H. W. H. Beyts, R.M.A. fell on 23rd June, until their arrival at Tientsin, 26th June, and was of the greatest assistance to Major Johnstone R.M.L.I.

Mr Arthur E. Cossey, assistant Engineer, HMS *Aurora*, at much risk to himself returned from our most advanced post towards Anting Station to bring important news.

Mr Clive Bigham, late Grenadier Guards, honorary attaché to HM Legation at Peking, has been attached to me as Intelligence Officer, and shown much zeal and ability as such; he has been of great value to me.

Mr Archibald Currie, C.E., B.Sc., resident engineer in charge of railway line between Tientsin and Peking, came with us to take charge of the trains and their personnel, and to repair the line. In this he worked with a skill and energy not to be surpassed. He acted in opposition to the Chinese director-in-chief of the railway, for our benefit, and HM Service and the Allies owe him a debt of gratitude which I submit must be acknowledged and repaid. He has lost his home and nearly all his worldly possessions out here, destroyed by the Chinese.

Mr C. W. Campbell, HM Consul for Wuchow (on leave) accompanied us as interpreter, and was of the utmost value by his knowledge both of the language and customs of the Chinese. He showed untiring zeal and I would submit him for the decided acknowledgements of HM Government.

When the fact of the Chinese having beheaded anyone they got is considered, the conduct of such officers or men as risked themselves to such capture, is to be praised far more than if against a civilised foe.

E. H. Seymour'

# OFFICERS NOT PRESENT WITH THE SEYMOUR EXPEDITION

Officers who were *not present* in the Seymour Expedition from ships supplying brigade (being named in the List of Naval and Marine Officers present in Tientsin between 10th and 26th June 1900 – *Affairs at Tientsin* – Letter No. 388 from Commander-in-Chief on the China Station, dated 8 July 1900)

**HMS** *Centurion*
Robert Kilpatrick
Edgar W. Riley
George H. Borrett
Colpoys C. Walcott
Cecil B. Prickett
John W. Dustan
William A. Harris

**HMS** *Aurora*
Edward H. Bayly
Thomas W. Kemp
George B. Powell
Charles D. Roper
Charles F. Ballard
Edward F. Power
Augustus P. Hughes
Francis C. Hanning-Lee
Robert H. Clark-Hall
Cecil R. Hemans
Henry C. Halahan
Arthur F. Crutchley

**HMS** *Orlando*
James H. T. Burke
Philip N. Wright
Herbert M. Perfect
Frederick C. Fisher
Edmond A. B. Stanley
George Gipps
John A. Collett
George W. Taylor
Dennis de C. A. Herbert
John H. Young

# OFFICERS LISTED AS PRESENT WITH THE SEYMOUR EXPEDITION

Officers listed in the *London Gazette* 5 October 1900 as being *present* with the Seymour Expedition. (Sixty-six names are given whereas in the same report Admiral Seymour refers to sixty-two officers. This may be that he counted the four marine officers in with the marines?)

**HMS** *Centurion*
Vice-Admiral Sir Edward H. Seymour, K.C.B.
Flag Lieutenant Fredk. A. Powlett
Secretary Francis C. Alton
Secretary's Clerk, Wm. G. Littlejohns
Secretary's Clerk, Henry W. E. Manisty
Flag Captain John R. Jellicoe (wounded 21 June, Peitsang)
Commander Charles D. Granville
Lieutenant George M. K. Fair
Lieutenant Edward G. Lowther-Crofton
Lieutenant John L. F. Luttrell
Lieutenant James M. Fairie
Lieutenant Wyndham L. Bamber (wounded 21 June, Peitsang)
Lieutenant Claud H. Sinclair
Major James R. Johnstone, R.M.L.I.
Captain Herbert W. H. Beyts, R.M.A. (killed 23 June, Hsiku)
Chaplain and Naval Instructor, Rev Ernest F. Harrison Smith M.A.
Fleet Surgeon Thomas M. Sibbald
Sub Lieutenant Morris E. Cochrane
Surgeon Edward B. Pickthorn
Assistant Paymaster Charles J. E. Rotter
Engineer George H. Cockey

Assistant Engineer George H. Starr
Acting Gunner Charles Davidge
Acting Gunner Frank Sammels
Carpenter James Attrill
Midshipman Hector Boyes
Midshipman Wm. B. C. Jones
Midshipman Charles D. Burke
   (wounded 21 June, Peitsang)

Midshipman Sydney Bailey HMS *Centurion*

Midshipman Sydney R. Bailey
Midshipman St. Andrew St. John
Midshipman Guy B. Alexander
Midshipman Hardinge L. Shepard
Midshipman Philip W. Douglas
Midshipman Robert L. Jermain
Midshipman Edward O. B. S. Osborne
Midshipman Frank O'B Wilson
   (wounded 21 June, Peitsang)
Midshipman John C. Davis
Augustus E. Tabuteau (wounded
   21 June, Peitsang) Clerk

**HMS *Aurora***
Lieutenant Arthur G. Smith
Captain Henry T. R. Lloyd, R.M.L.I.
Assistant Engineer Arthur E. Cossey
Midshipman Thomas R. Fforde
Midshipman Charles B. Dickson
Midshipman George M. Hill

**HMS *Orlando***
Lieutenant Francis E. M. Garforth
Assistant Paymaster Edward F. Murray
Gunner Patrick McGuire
Midshipman Cloudesley V. Robinson
Midshipman Herbert F. Littledale
Midshipman Charles P. Dumaresq

**HMS *Endymion***
Commander William O. Boothby
Lieutenant Horatio W. Colomb
   (wounded 21 June, Peitsang –
   and 27 June, Tientsin Arsenal)
Lieutenant Frank Powell
Captain Richard O. M. Doig, R.M.L.I.
Chaplain, Rev John C. Leishman
Sub Lieutenant Lawrence W. Braithwaite
   (wounded 22 June, Hsiku)
Surgeon Eric D. Macnamara, B.A.
Engineer Ethelbert S. Silk
Midshipman Henry J. S. Brownrigg
Midshipman Guy D. Fanshawe
Midshipman Edwin A. Homan
Midshipman Norman M. C. Thurston
Midshipman Francis S. McGachen
Midshipman Herbert R. McClure
Midshipman Stuart E. Holder

## FIGHTING STRENGTHS

|  | Guns | Officers | Men | Commanded by |
|---|---|---|---|---|
| Austria | 2 | 1 | 24 | Lieut. Prochasca |
| British | 1 6-pdr Hotch QF | 62 | 640 |  |
|  | 3 9-pdr M.L. |  | 213 (marines) | Vice-Admiral Sir |
|  | 2 .45 Maxim |  |  | E. H. Seymour K.C.B. |
|  | 6.45 Nord. |  |  |  |
| France | 1 Field Gun | 7 | 151 | Captain de Marolles |
| Germany | 2 Maxim | 23 | 427 | Captain von Usedom |
| Italy | 1 Maxim | 2 | 38 | Lieutenant Sirianni |
| Japan | — | 2 | 52 | Captain Mori |
| Russia | 1 Field Gun | 7 | 305 | Commander Chagkin |
| U.S.A. | 1 13-pdr | 6 | 106 | Captain B. H. McCalla |
|  | 1 Colt auto |  |  |  |

Making a total force of 110 officers, 1,956 men and 19 guns.

## CASUALTY LIST

**BRITISH**

|  |  |  |
|---|---|---|
| HMS *Centurion* | Officers wounded | 5 |
|  | Seamen, etc. killed | 9 |
|  | Seamen, etc. wounded | 36 |
|  | Marine officers killed | 1 |
|  | Marines killed | 6 |
|  | Marines wounded | 7 |
| HMS *Aurora* | Seamen, etc. wounded | 2 |
|  | Marines killed | 3 |
|  | Marines wounded | 5 |
| HMS *Orlando* | Seamen, etc. killed | 1 |
|  | Seamen, etc. wounded | 13 |
| HMS *Endymion* | Officers wounded | 3 |
|  | Seamen, etc. killed | 5 |
|  | Seamen, etc. wounded | 15 |
|  | Marines killed | 5 |
|  | Marines wounded | 6 |
| Wei Hai Wei Detachment |  |  |
|  | Marines wounded | 5 |
|  |  | 127 |

**ALLIES**

|  |  |  |
|---|---|---|
| Austria | Seamen, etc. killed | 1 |
|  | Seamen, etc. wounded | 1 |
| France | Seamen, etc. killed | 1 |

|         |                      |     |
|---------|----------------------|-----|
|         | Seamen, etc. wounded | 10  |
| Germany | Officers killed      | 1   |
|         | Officers wounded     | 6   |
|         | Seamen, etc. killed  | 11  |
|         | Seamen, etc. wounded | 56  |
| Italy   | Seamen, etc. killed  | 5   |
|         | Seamen, etc. wounded | 3   |
| Japan   | Seamen, etc. killed  | 2   |
|         | Seamen, etc. wounded | 3   |
| Russia  | Officers wounded     | 4   |
|         | Seamen, etc. killed  | 10  |
|         | Seamen, etc. wounded | 23  |
| U.S.A.  | Officers wounded     | 2   |
|         | Seamen, etc. killed  | 4   |
|         | Seamen, etc. wounded | 25  |
|         |                      | 295 |

*Summary*: 2 officers and 63 men killed; 20 officers and 210 men wounded making a grand total of 295 officers and men killed and wounded.

# LOG ENTRIES OF SHIPS CONCERNED
## RELATING TO THE LANDING OF MEN FOR FIGHTING AT THE TIME OF THE SEYMOUR EXPEDITION.

**HMS *Centurion***
*June 1*
1252 at single anchor off Taku.
*June 4*
Sent machine gun crew and gun and Sub Lieut. Cochrane to *Whiting* for duty at Tientsin.
1720 landing parties preparing accoutrements.
*June 5*
Field and Maxim gun crew at drill. P.M. B and C companies preparing for landing (little later but no time given) Sent B and C companies to Taku, Commander Granville in command. Working top searchlight for signal purposes.
*June 6*
0800 Sent R.M. detachment to Taku. P.M. mustered A company in heavy marching order. P.M. burnt searchlight for signalling ('burnt' meaning 'lit' in naval terms).
*June 9*
P.M. landing one Maxim on tripod with crew and ammunition. Late P.M. prepared for landing A and D companies.
*July 10*
Early A.M. landed A and D companies, two field guns and one 6-pdr.
*June 22*
P.M. landed one Maxim on tripod with carriage and 8,000 rounds and Lieut. Borrett and twelve men. (Lieut. Borrett had not been engaged in the Taku Forts battle, and it is likely the gun's crew were landed for action for the first time too).

**HMS *Aurora***
*June 7*
Anchored off Taku, prepared to land two companies and three field guns with crews fully equipped. 2040 very heavy rain, squall and continuous vivid lightning.
*June 8*
Preparing for landing small arm men, field guns and crews and R.M. detachment.
*June 9*
A.M. *Fame* closed squadron from Taku. 1600 landed Capt. T. Lloyd and seventy-eight marines equipped for service.
*June 10*
0140 landed two small arm companies, three field guns and crews equipped for service with provisions and stores in charge of Captain E. H. Bayly, R.N.
*June 12*
A.M. discharged for passage to Naval Force five ratings. P.M. sent stores and provisions for landed force.

HMS *Endymion*

## HMS *Endymion*

*June 2*
1745 anchored off Taku. Found here *Centurion* (Flag), *Orlando, Fame, Whiting*.
*June 3*
1600 landing party fell in. Packed field and machine gun limbers.
*June 4*
Exercised landing party aboard A.M. and P.M.
*June 6*
1000 *Fame* took in landing party of marines from Flagship.
*June 7*
Exercised small arm companies and marines at divisional gun drill.
*June 9*
2340 prepared for landing.
*June 10*
Sent landing party consisting of two rifle companies of twenty file each, all marines. two 9-pdr. field guns crews and two Nordenfeldt .45 machine guns crews under Commander Boothby with Lieuts Colomb, and Powell. Capt Doig R.M.L.I., Sub Lt. Braithwaite, Midshipmen Brownrigg, Fanshawe, Homan, Robinson, Thurston, McClure, McGachan, and Holder in *Fame*. Launch being towed in by steam pinnace with guns. Picket boat towed in *Aurora*'s boats. 0830 one stoker returned, injured from landing party.

## HMS *Orlando*

*May 30*
1319 came to single anchor at Taku Bar. Saluted Chinese country, Chinese, Russian and

American admirals; Chinese, Russian and American flagships returned salute. Found in harbour four Russian, one American, one French, one Italian and one Chinese men of war.

*May 31*
0130 landed sixty-five seamen and five officers equipped for active service.

*June 7*
Stokers to pistol drill.

*June 10*
Landed ninety-six officers and men and two machine guns for active service. Crew employed getting up provisions for naval brigade. Landed one officer, two men and seven days provisions for 150 men.

*June 13*
One Pte R.M.L.I. returned on board from Naval Brigade. Captain Burke, Mid. Young, seven rates and two 6-pdr QF guns landed for service with naval brigade (could only have been used in Tientsin – contact with brigade lost).

# MEDALS TO MEN OF THE SEYMOUR EXPEDITION

The problem is that while 'Defence of Legations' and 'Taku Forts' bars clearly identify a recipient to an action, the bar 'Relief of Pekin' covers a number of events. A recipient may have taken part in most of those events, or only one of them.

While the Germans had fourteen bars for major battles of the campaign, the British 'Relief of Pekin' bar did duty for 'all those engaged in the operations on shore at or beyond Taku for the Relief of Pekin, between 10th June and 14th August 1900, both dates inclusive'.

Seymour's Expedition started out on 10 June. Then, following the battle of the Taku Forts, a naval brigade moved forward to relieve Tientsin. As the 'Taku Forts' bar was for 17 June it means that those entitled to both that and 'Relief of Pekin' could not have been on the Seymour Expedition, which had left a week earlier and was by 17 June itself cut off.

A brigade next moved out of Tientsin to rescue Admiral Seymour. Then came very severe actions in Tientsin and finally the brigade that moved out for the actual relief of Pekin. This last expedition we know had 200 bluejackets of which one hundred belonged to HMS *Terrible*, thirty-five to *Endymion* and five to *Aurora*, and included men from *Centurion*. There were also 300 marines (Commission of HMS *Terrible*).

What can be said with certainty is that the naval brigade of Seymour's Expedition came from only four ships and one shore establishment and that the medal rolls give single 'Relief of Pekin' bare entitlements to their complements as follows:

| | |
|---|---:|
| HMS *Centurion* | 392 |
| HMS *Aurora* | 256 |
| HMS *Orlando* | 187 |
| HMS *Endymion* | 282 |
| Wei Hai Wei (marines) | 72 |
| | 1,189 |

It is also known that there were 915 British in the expedition. So we are left with the tantalising position that 274 out of 1,189 men could not have taken part in the expedition.

Fortunately, David Beatty's diary helps us identify the whereabouts of a large proportion of this number. His diary entry for 11 June (Monday) reads:

'We soon had the men settled down with plenty of straw-matting, while the officers were billeted at different private houses, the civilians being exceedingly hospitable. We found in the Godowns 120 of the *Aurora*'s men, all Bluejackets, under Lieutenant Powell. There were also in the settlement in a Godown in Victoria Road, a detachment of one hundred men and twenty-eight marines under Lieutenant Wright of *Orlando*, which brought the British force in Tientsin up to 430 men and officers to defend the British Settlement.'

This must mean that the majority of both *Aurora* and *Orlando*'s men served in Tientsin with only 136 from Aurora and fifty-nine from *Orlando* taking part in Seymour's Expedition. Apart from the officers, whose whereabouts are all known, and a handful of men named in despatches, etc., it is therefore unlikely that medals to these ships can be attributed to the Seymour Expedition with any confidence until more information comes to light. Perhaps one positive statement can be that no marines from *Orlando* were on the expedition (there are twenty-eight on the medal roll and David Beatty places all twenty-eight in Tientsin).

However, only twenty-six men have to be accounted for to ensure reasonably accurate attribution for all the other ships, etc., who supplied a total of 746 men for the expedition.

There is no evidence to suggest that the Wei Hai Wei detachment served in any other theatre of operations until the expedition was over and therefore, unless some such information comes to light, it appears safe to assume all Wei Hai Wei bars 'Relief of Pekin' belong to the Seymour Expedition. This likelihood is enhanced by our ability to account for the twenty-six missing men elsewhere.

It is noteworthy that no officers from HMS *Endymion* were present at Tientsin (List of Naval and Marine Officers present in Tientsin between 10th and 26th June 1900) and it is therefore likely that the entire brigade from *Endymion* was present with Seymour. However, Clowes' (*The Royal Navy*) table of casualties at Tientsin up to 26 June includes one man from HMS *Endymion* as wounded. This may be explained by an entry in *Endymion*'s log showing a stoker returned having been injured during the landing on 10 June.

The unaccounted twenty-six men can be placed as follows:

There are *seven* named *Centurion* officers listed as being present in Tientsin during the Seymour Expedition. One of these, Lieutenant G. H. Borrett took *twelve* men (Log entry 22 June) to Tientsin from *Centurion*. (It is always possible that the men had also fought at Taku Forts, but unlikely as that naval force had already moved to the relief of Tientsin under Commander Cradock. Borrett did not take part in the battle of the Taku Forts.)

Another log entry – from HMS *Orlando* – tells us that on 13 June Captain Burke, Midshipman Young and seven ratings landed for service with the Naval Brigade from HMS *Orlando*. (They could not have got further than Tientsin and they were not part of the number recorded in Beatty's diary, as that entry was on 11 June).

Already then we have accounted for more than twenty-six names – but as every student of military history knows, military numbers seldom actually agree exactly! Also we know of three civilians who accompanied the expedition though their names do not appear on the rolls.

The probability therefore is that there is a ninety-nine per cent chance that any 'Relief of Pekin' bar to HMS *Endymion* can be attributed to Seymour's Expedition; and that only twelve unknown names out of the medal roll of 392 for *Centurion*, did not serve on the expedition.

# HMS *Aurora* Relief of Peking bar

| Number | Name | Rank/Rating |
|---|---|---|
| 155018 | Algar, S. G. | A.B. |
| PLY 6282 | Armstrong, W. F. | Lance Corp., R.M. (D) |
| PLY 8820 | Ashley, C. R. | Pte., R.M. |
| PO 8302 | Arnold, W. | Pte., R.M. (P) |
| 177886 | Bayly, E. H. | Captain, R.N. |
| 188482 | Ballard, C. F. | Lt. R.N. (D) |
| 185119 | Bell, John | A.B. |
| 191083 | Berriball, W. A. | Ord. |
| 185210 | Bowles, J. J. S. | A.B. |
| 180843 | Blackmore, C. | Ord. |
| 180256 | Bate, A. | Ord. |
| 189335 | Bryant, A. | A.B. |
| 193915 | Blatchford, J. D. | A.B. |
| 182060 | Barrett, J. | Ord. (D) |
| 118088 | Bates, R. | Ord. |
| 191622 | Burke, B. | A.B. |
| 189145 | Berry, E. J. | Ord. |
| 95296 | Bosley, W. W. | P.O. 2nd Class |
| 341806 | Boland, A. | Blacksmith's Mate |
| PLY 6094 | Barrett, J. | Cpl., R.M. |
| PLY 5148 | Brown, A. J. | Cpl., R.M. |
| PLY 8670 | Bowden, W. | Pte., R.M. |
|  | Bury, C. W. | Asst. Engineer |
| 127983 | Cossey, A. E. | Mid. |
| 118063 | Clark-Hall, R. H. | P.O. 1st Class |
| 187550 | Collins, D. | P.O. 2nd Class |
| 162488 | Carroll, P. | Ord. |
| 126205 | Cole, W. J. | A.B. |
| 184275 | Cudd, J. A. | A.B. |
| 181445 | Collins, J. H. | A.B. |
| 181450 | Cotter, P. | A.B. |
| 193925 | Currell, J. H. | A.B. (D) |
| 193913 | Chalet, E. F. | A.B. |
| 193917 | Carley, M. | Ord. |
| 179796 | Connolly, M. | A.B. |
| 341233 | Connelly, T. | A.B. |
|  | Cousins, A. | Arm's Crew |
|  | Cook, A. J. |  |
| PLY 7685 | Cook, W. J. | Bugler, R.M. |
| PLY 7129 | Collins, W. J. | Pte., R.M. |
| PLY 8816 | Cooper, W. | Pte., R.M. |
| PLY 8826 | Culverwell, H. | Pte., R.M. |
| PLY 8529 | Cree, G. B. | Sgt., R.M. (P) |
| PLY 4978 | Cooper, G. F. | P.O. 1st Class |
| 138720 | Collings, W. S. |  |
| 190093 | Dickson, C. B. | Mid. (P) |
| 183407 | Docking, C. | Ord. |
| 183764 | Dunn, D. | A.B. |
| 180334 | Donovan, D. | A.B. |
| 194516 | Driscoll, M. | A.B. |
| 193912 | Dale, S. G. | A.B. |
| 189083 | Deasey, J. | A.B. |
| 268434 | Drown, T. | E.R.A. 3rd Class |
| PLY 8214 | Day, J. W. | Pte., R.M. |
| PLY 5816 | Dring, C. D. | Pte., R.M. (DD) |
|  | Davies, T. |  |
| 186004 | Edwards, L. | A.B. |
| 191151 | Endacott, A. B. | A.B. |
| PLY 5317 | Eden, J. | Pte., R.M. |
| PLY 4814 | Eddiford, H. | Pte., R.M. (DD) |
| 193353 | Filewood, W. F. | Qdk. Sig. (D) |
| 185951 | Finn, P. | A.B. |
| 183776 | Flynn, P. | Ord. |
| 194023 | Flood, J. | Ord. |
| 194492 | Finnemore, J. L. | Ord. (D) |
| 192620 | Freebury, E. | A.B. |
| 180845 | Flynn, P. | Cpl., R.M. |
| PLY 6830 | Fielding, J. | Pte., R.M. |
| PLY 7805 | Farrant, W. H. | Lance Corp., R.M. |
| PLY 5125 | Frary, W. | Pte., R.M. |
| PLY 4292 | Fogden, T. | Pte., R.M. |
| PLY 8516 | Fishlock, G. T. |  |
| 151923 | Gonterias, E. F. | A.B. |
| 177870 | Gates, W. J. | Ldg. Seaman |
| 183400 | Gorman, T. | Ord. |
| 193908 | Geogeon, W. | A.B. |

30

| Number | Name | Rank/Rating |
|---|---|---|
| 153942 | Gagg, C. | A.B. |
| 268356 | Gunn, E. | E.R.A. 3rd Class |
| 160745 | Gribble, E. J. | Stoker |
| | Hughes, A. P. | Asst. Paymaster |
| | Hemans, C. R. | Mid. |
| | Halahan, H. C. | Mid. |
| | Hill, G. M. | Mid. |
| | Hanning-Lee, F. C. | |
| 150850 | Huxham, R. J. | Ldg. Seaman |
| 152164 | Hodges, H. | P.O. 1st Class |
| 157987 | Hill, A. | Ldg. Seaman |
| 157301 | Hooper, G. | A.B. |
| 179631 | Hingston, C. | A.B. |
| 180000 | Honey, W. E. T. | A.B. |
| 180711 | Hill, C. | Ord. |
| 194508 | Hambly, F. | A.B. (D) |
| 189344 | Hornibrook, J. | Ord. |
| 168752 | Hickey, J. J. | 2nd Yeo. Sigs. |
| 192545 | Horn, G. | Ord. |
| 191503 | Hann, W. F. | Ord. |
| 197900 | Henstone, A. E. | Ord. |
| 159888 | Hanning, J. | Ldg. Shipt |
| PLY 5935 | Hurford, A. | Act. Sgt., R.M. |
| PLY 6863 | Hall, H. F. | Lance Sgt., R.M. (D) |
| PLY 8831 | Hunt, G. S. | Pte., R.M. |
| PLY 8828 | Helyar, J. | Pte., R.M. |
| PLY 4266 | Hansell, A. E. | Pte., R.M. |
| PLY 8450 | Haylock, W. | Pte., R.M. |
| CH 10298 | Hutton, R. J. | Lance Corp., R.M. |
| CH 11032 | Humphrey, G. H. | Pte., R.M. |
| CH 9064 | Heath, B. W. | P.O. 1st Class (P) |
| 131455 | Hayes, John | |
| 158918 | Jarvis, J. H. | P.O. 2nd Class |
| 183866 | Jones, H. | A.B. |
| 182081 | Johnson, W. | A.B. |
| 180588 | James, E. S. | A.B. |
| 194497 | Jarman, C. H. | Ord. (P) |
| 119472 | Jackson, R. | Ldg. Seaman |
| 173966 | Johnson, P. | A.B. (D) |
| PLY 8602 | Jenkins, H. | Pte., R.M. (D) |
| 143440 | Kingcome, W. W. | A.B. |
| 184229 | Kinver, J. | A.B. |
| 156151 | Kingsley, J. | A.B. (P) |
| 181253 | Keogh, P. J. | A.B. |
| 135139 | Kelly, J. | Stoker |
| | Lloyd, H. T. R. | Captain, R.M.L.I. (DD) |
| 90605 | Lunt, W. O. | C.P.O. |
| 155287 | Libby, T. | P.O. 2nd Class |
| 165524 | Luxton, W. | Ldg. Seaman |
| 190608 | Loughran, A. | A.B. (D) |
| 158982 | Lewis, F. G. | A.B. |
| 189075 | Lapidge, J. E. | Ord. |
| 179593 | Lang, W. J. | A.B. |
| 193934 | Lynch, T. | A.B. |
| 193921 | Lane, J. | A.B. (D) |
| 195722 | Lamerton, A. J. G. | Ord. |
| 194509 | Lavers, G. | Ord. (D) |
| 156802 | Le Scelleur, G. H. | A.B. |
| 278306 | Lee, W. J. | Stoker |
| PLY 5436 | Luxton, W. J. | Pte., R.M. |
| 150967 | Moynihan, J. | P.O. 1st Class |
| 128006 | Martin, W. T. | P.O. 1st Class |
| 123729 | Moore, C. H. | P.O. 1st Class |
| 183765 | Murphy, J. | A.B. |
| 180664 | Molesworth, F. G. | Ldg. Seaman |
| 192195 | Mayle, W. | A.B. |
| 193910 | McCarthy, J. | A.B. |
| 169473 | McGee, G. T. | A.B. |
| 188479 | Mole, F. W. | A.B. |
| 194127 | Mitchell J. E. | Ord. |
| 192585 | Murch, A. E. | Ord. |
| 127173 | Maunder, C. | Ldg. Seaman |
| 173167 | Mitchell, E. F. J. | Qdk. Sig. |
| 197888 | McCracken, J. T. | Ord. |
| 287132 | Morgan, J. | Stoker |
| 283540 | McAllister, E. | Stoker |
| | Moo, A. H. | Dom. 2nd Class |
| PLY 8817 | Mitchell, F. G. | Pte., R.M. |
| PLY 8833 | Mutch, W. G. | Pte., R.M. |
| PLY 8838 | McCabe, B. | Pte., R.M. |

| | | |
|---|---|---|
| PLY 6409 | McGuigan, A. | Pte., R.M. |
| PLY 8395 | Mitchell, H. | Pte., R.M. |
| 184887 | Neil, E. | A.B. |
| 180740 | Noonan, W. | A.B. |
| 185784 | Nolan, W. | A.B. (D) |
| 180276 | Nelmes, A. E. | A.B. |
| 191402 | Northcott, G. R. | Pte., R.M. |
| PLY 6824 | Nelson, F. | |
| 158359 | O'Callaghan, J. | A.B. |
| 189676 | Oldrieve, L. | Ord. |
| 192179 | Orley, G. C. | Ord. |
| | Powell, G. B. | Lieut., R.N. |
| 156761 | Power, E. F. | Surgeon |
| 178330 | Prew, H. | A.B. |
| 184641 | Prynn, T. | A.B. |
| 194494 | Piggott, J. E. | A.B. |
| 193923 | Perring, W. | Ord. |
| 188251 | Power, W. | A.B. |
| 185723 | Price, W. | Ord. |
| 280056 | Parsonage, W. | A.B. (P) |
| 276189 | Perrin, W. J. | Stoker |
| 288568 | Ponsford, F. | Stoker |
| | Parsons, J. E. | Stoker |
| PLY 5059 | Poi, A. L. | Dom. 3rd Class |
| PLY 8818 | Prosser, A. | Pte., R.M. |
| | Powell, J. | Pte., R.M. |
| 98448 | Quincey, W. | P.O. 1st Class |
| | Roper, C. D. | Lieut., R.N. |
| 166592 | Rea, J. | P.O. 2nd Class |
| 183136 | Robinson, C. M. V. | A.B. |
| 179431 | Russell, H. E. | A.B. |
| 184029 | Revatta, T. | A.B. |
| 184496 | Richards, W. J. | A.B. |
| 181201 | Rendle, J. R. | Ord. |
| 194507 | Roskruge, S. | A.B. |
| 191484 | Rew, A. H. | Ord. |
| 288593 | Rodda, S. A. | Stoker |
| 141518 | Rooke, H. W. | Armourer |
| 163967 | Rayner, G. H. | S.B. Stwd. |
| CH 9042 | Randall, H. G. | Pte., R.M. |
| | Smith, A. G. | Lieut., R.N. |
| | Sams, C. H. H. | Mid. |
| | Syson, J. L. | Asst. Clerk (D) |
| 111305 | Sullivan, J. | P.O. 1st Class |
| 126994 | Shore, W. R. E. | A.B. |
| 132146 | Spear, W. | P.O. 2nd Class |
| 120900 | Sly, T. N. | P.O. 1st Class |
| 183864 | Smith, L. | A.B. |
| 180025 | Stribley, R. | A.B. |
| 176092 | Spry, A. V. | A.B. |
| 179757 | Shea, R. | A.B. |
| 187803 | Spillane, J. | Ord. |
| 181219 | Stevens, A. C. | A.B. |
| 157855 | Skinner, R. | A.B. |
| 192238 | Scoble, J. H. | Ord. |
| 179656 | Skinner, W. C. | A.B. |
| 159703 | Steer, C. E. S. | A.B. |
| 191703 | Sanders, R. | Ord. |
| 183127 | Squire, D. | Qdk. Sig. |
| 283293 | Shanahan, J. | Stoker |
| 288579 | Sercombe, E. R. | Stoker |
| 288590 | Scully, E. W. | Stoker |
| PLY 7652 | Stowell, A. | Pte., R.M. |
| PLY 5611 | Strain, P. | Pte., R.M. |
| PLY 8814 | Shepherd, J. | Pte., R.M. (P) |
| PLY 8216 | Staughton, A. W. | Cpl., R.M. (P) |
| PLY 7704 | Sharp, E. | Pte., R.M. |
| PLY 7390 | Sumpter, T. E. | Pte., R.M. |
| CH 8945 | Seddon, J. W. | Pte., R.M. |
| | Sam, A. | Dom. 3rd Class |
| 111337 | Townsend, A. | P.O. 1st Class |
| 193930 | Toohey, W. | Ord. |
| 193355 | Taylor, F. E. | Ord. |
| 191624 | Tancock, S. J. | A.B. |
| 342322 | Tredant, J. V. | Carp.'s Crew |
| PLY 5075 | Toyer, W. | Pte., R.M. |
| PLY 6428 | Taylor, A. | Pte., R.M. |

| | | |
|---|---|---|
| 126852 | Taylor, T. H. | P.O. 1st Class |
| 144659 | Williams, A. E. | P.O. 1st Class |
| 165566 | Wakeham, W. G. | P.O. 2nd Class |
| 183977 | Williamson, C. H. | A.B. (D) |
| 184156 | Wills, J. C. | A.B. |
| 186238 | Wardle, G. H. | A.B. |
| 147419 | Wright, R. W. | A.B. |
| 188267 | Ward, W. R. | A.B. |
| 193933 | Williams, P. | A.B. |
| 194520 | Webber, H. H. | A.B. |
| 194515 | Webb, F. J. | Ord. |
| 192502 | Wheeler, W. J. | Ord. |
| 192579 | Wills, W. | A.B. |
| 191135 | Willmott, J. R. | Ord. |
| 153231 | Wakem, J. | Act. Chief Stoker |
| 159535 | Williams, J. | Stoker |
| PLY 8762 | Wiseman, H. E. | Pte., R.M. |
| PLY 8839 | Wynn, W. J. | Pte., R.M. |
| PLY 7538 | Wickham, H. | Pte., R.M. |
| PO 6918 | Webb, G. T. R. | A.B. |
| J47090 | Yalland, J. P. | |
| PLY 2515 | Young, A. | Pte., R.M. |

## HMS *Centurion*

| | | |
|---|---|---|
| | Alton, F. C. | Secretary (P) |
| 139203 | Attrill, J. | Chief Carp. (P) |
| 148437 | Alexander, G. B. | Mid. |
| 185840 | Atkinson, B. G. | A.B. |
| 190246 | Adams, J. J. A. E. | Ldg. Seaman |
| 281871 | Attwood, J. | A.B. |
| 281904 | Ashby, H. | A.B. |
| CH 8242 | Armstrong, T. | Stoker |
| | Allott, J. | Stoker |
| | Amos, W. | Pte., R.M. |
| | Bigham, C. C. | Lt. (Army) A.D.C. to Admiral |
| | Bamber, W. L. | Lieut., R.M. |
| | Burke, C. D. | Mid. |
| | Boyes, H. | Mid. |
| | Bailey, S. R. | Mid. (P) |
| 183036 | Borrett, G. H. | Lieut. |
| 183246 | Beyts, H. W. H. | Captain., R.M.A. |
| 176923 | Bastard, G. E. | A.B. |
| 176279 | Brett, B. | A.B. |
| 183251 | Beach, H. G. | Ldg. Seaman |
| 183480 | Bartlett, F. A. | A.B. |
| 151601 | Baillie, W. K. | A.B. |
| 143494 | Bevis, A. | A.B. |
| 151101 | Burford, A. A. | A.B. |
| 179316 | Burton, G. R. J. | P.O. 1st Class |
| 179328 | Bamford, J. G. | Ldg. Seaman |
| 157615 | Barnes, A. H. | A.B. |
| 158529 | Balcomb, G. | A.B. |
| 186409 | Brown, W. G. | A.B. |
| 184682 | Bone, S. H. | A.B. |
| 184684 | Baxter, W. | A.B. |
| 181778 | Batchelor, W. | A.B. |
| 185001 | Bone, E. R. | Qdk. Sig. |
| 184597 | Bromley, C. W. | A.B. (P) |
| 138849 | Bigg, F. W. | A.B. |
| 193635 | Benewith, A. | P.O. 1st Class |
| 198639 | Bentley, W. D. B. | A.B. (P) |
| 191559 | Baker, G. W. | Ord. |
| 183671 | Bryson, J. | A.B. |
| 191847 | Breeds, F. | Ord. (DD) |
| 191593 | Bolton, H. S. | A.B. |
| 160779 | Bromley, J. | A.B. |
| 193432 | Brown, A. E. | Ldg. Sig. |
| 197207 | Butler, W. R. | Ord. (P) |
| 154373 | Button, H. | A.B. |
| 280742 | Bundy, A. C. | P.O. 2nd Class |
| 175921 | Bradley, J. W. | Stoker |
| 282127 | Blackman, F. L. | Ldg. Stoker 2nd Class |
| 280508 | Butler, F. | Stoker |
| 128350 | Beale, H. | Ldg. Stoker 2nd Class |
| 286629 | Bartle, H. | Ldg. Stoker 1st Class |
| 269360 | Bastable, F. | Stoker (P) |
| 281985 | Brien, J. | E.R.A. 4th Class |
| 149838 | Barker, B. | Stoker |
| 128533 | Brown, F. | Stoker (DD) |
| | Beaumont, A. | Act. Armourer |
| | Burnett, A. | |

| Number | Name | Rating |
|---|---|---|
| 340374 | Bridges, G. | Blacksmith's Mate |
| 341474 | Brown, G. J. | Painter 2nd Class |
| PO 8292 | Burns, R. | Pte., R.M. |
| RMA 5780 | Bairne, J. | Gunner R.M.A. |
| RMA 5657 | Brooks, H. | Gunner R.M.A. |
| RMA 5735 | Bull, T. | Gunner R.M.A. (D) |
| PO 8241 | Bailey, A. | Pte., R.M. |
| RMA 4819 | Bubb, J. | Gunner R.M.A. |
| PLY 2762 | Bowman, J. | Sgt., R.M. |
| CHA 5442 | Bruce, G. H. | Cpl., R.M. |
| 103747 | Cockey, G. H. | Engineer (P) |
| 183242 | Cochrane, M. E. | Sub. Lieut. |
| 138490 | Clark, G. | A.B. |
| 121994 | Compton, A. | A.B. |
| 147340 | Coombes, J. R. | Ldg. Seaman |
| 156093 | Clayton, W. | A.B. |
| 166230 | Coldwell, W. C. | A.B. |
| 124133 | Castle, E. W. | A.B. |
| 161530 | Clifford, P. | A.B. |
| 178643 | Chapman, W. C. | P.O. 1st Class |
| 184373 | Cornwell, J. | A.B. |
| 186961 | Cook, W. S. | A.B. |
| 186252 | Cufley, J. | A.B. |
| 192392 | Coulstock, F. | A.B. (D) |
| 185827 | Cockerill, H. B. | A.B. (P) |
| 196191 | Cottam, S. | A.B. |
| 152899 | Cooper, W. | P.O. 2nd Class |
| 281184 | Coleman, W. | Stoker |
| 281304 | Cooper, R. E. | Stoker |
| 280520 | Catt, J. | Stoker (DD) |
| 281886 | Cresdee, W. J. | Stoker |
| 277206 | Clayton, J. | Ldg. Stoker 2nd Class (P) |
| 282957 | Cruickshank, J. | Stoker |
| 154257 | Currie, S. | Ldg. Stoker 1st Class (D) |
| 282964 | Caven, W. | Stoker |
| 143242 | Caller, H. J. | Armourer |
| RMA 5705 | Corbett, G. C. | Gunner R.M.A. (P) |
| RMA 5734 | Curtis, J. W. | Gunner R.M.A. |
| 127826 | Callaway, H. C. B. | P.O. 1st Class |
|  | Clapson, G. H. |  |
|  | Crosse, W. H. |  |
| 150763 | Douglas, P. W. | Mid. (D) |
| 162423 | Davidge, C. | Act. Gunner |
| 110673 | Davis, J. C. | Mid. (P) |
| 184706 | Derkin, J. H. | P.O. 2nd Class |
| 171600 | Davison, W. J. | A.B. |
| 185736 | Davies, J. | A.B. |
| 282143 | Davey, J. E. | A.B. |
| RMA 5769 | Davis, J. C. | 2nd Yeo. Sigs. |
| RMA 3498 | Devine, T. | Qdk. Sig. |
| PO 6212 | Dinwoodie, J. | Stoker (P) |
|  | Duly, W. K. | Gunner, R.M.A. |
|  | Davies, W. H. | Sgt., R.M.A. (P) |
|  | Durrant, C. | Pte., R.M. |
| 185496 | Ellis, G. | Boatswain (P) |
| 186974 | Eley, W. | A.B. |
| 192009 | Emery, E. W. | A.B. |
| 157115 | Edney, H. C. | Ldg. Sig. |
| 185512 | Emery, H. | Sig. |
| 196970 | Eccleston, T. | Ord. (D) |
| 281914 | Engholm, F. W. | Stoker (DD) |
| 282137 | Edbury, C. | Stoker |
| 281659 | Edwards, W. | Plumber's Mate |
| 341290 | Evans, T. A. | Bugler (D) |
| CH 8151 | Erskine, T. | Pte., R.M. (DD) |
| PO 8634 | Edwards, J. L. |  |
|  | Ellis, A. E. |  |
| 169195 | Farie, J. U. | Lieut. |
| 137944 | Fair, G. M. K. | Lieut. |
| 125018 | Foreman, A. G. | P.O. 1st Class (P) |
| 149450 | Ford, F. A. | A.B. |
| 281436 | Fryer, G. T. | A.B. |
| 192128 | French, H. | Ldg. Stoker 1st Class |
| 292475 | Floyd, E. | Stoker (P) |
| 343707 | Frost, E. | Stoker |
| 340877 | Finch, T. | Carp's Crew |
| PO 5715 | Fifield, W. E. | Cook's Mate |
| PO 3599 | Few, E. | Pte., R.M. (D) |
| PO 8250 | Ford, F. | Pte., R.M. |
|  | Frisby, E. | Pte., R.M. |
|  | Felton, I. | Dom. 3rd Class |
|  | Fat, A. H. |  |

| | | | |
|---|---|---|---|
| 177218 | Granville, C. D. | Capt's Mate (P) | |
| 183248 | Greavett, F. W. W. | Ldg. Shipt. | |
| 150929 | Griffiths, W. E. | Dom. 2nd Class | |
| 154106 | Goulding, J. | A.B. | Pte., R.M. |
| 184686 | Greening, R. | A.B. | Gunner R.M.A. |
| 185812 | Gardener, W. J. | A.B. | Gunner R.M.A. |
| 184996 | Gosford, H. | A.B. | Pte., R.M. |
| 162918 | Goodban, J. | Ldg. Seaman (P) | Pte., R.M. (DD) |
| 188610 | Gay, G. | A.B. | |
| 183696 | Gardner, D. C. | A.B. | |
| 183963 | Gathercole, E. | A.B. | |
| 191544 | Garnett, W. | A.B. | |
| 186978 | Green, G. A. | A.B. | |
| 280845 | Gambling, J. | Ldg. Stoker 2nd Class (P) | |
| 152679 | Greasley, G. W. | Ldg. Stoker 1st Class | |
| 282044 | Gosling, C. | Stoker | |
| 128492 | Gale, C. G. | Dom. 1st Class | |
| PO 8243 | Goldfinch, A. | Pte., R.M. | |
| PO 8245 | Gage, W. | Pte., R.M. | |
| RMA 5730 | Guy, A. | Gunner R.M.A. | |
| RMA 3257 | Goldstein, L. | Act. Bdr., R.M.A. | |
| PLY 5107 | Gainsley, J. H. | Sgt., R.M. (P) | |
| | Gunn, S. | | |
| 149661 | Hanmore, C. W. | A.B. | |
| 150891 | Hosier, T. W. | A.B. | |
| 148724 | Hipple, H. | A.B. | |
| 102268 | Hucker, A. E. B. | A.B. | |
| 152212 | Hayhow, R. J. | A.B. (Dup) | |
| 179696 | Harcourt, T. | A.B. | |
| 184696 | Hamilton, G. C. | A.B. | |
| 180094 | Hood, C. T. | A.B. | |
| 184732 | Horscroft, C. B. | A.B. | |
| 186982 | Hornigold, H. | A.B. | |
| 184736 | Hagger, E. C. | A.B. (D) | |
| 184998 | Hart, W. H. | E.R.A. 3rd Class | |
| 268402 | House, W. H. | Stoker | |
| 281186 | Hamer, A. V. | Stoker | |
| 280714 | Harris, C. H. | Stoker | |
| 283730 | Henderson, J. | Stoker | |
| 280093 | Horgan, F. | Stoker | |
| 281586 | Hewitt, R. W. | Stoker | |
| 158057 | Hellyer, A. J. | A.B. | |
| 164080 | Herring, E. | Stoker (D) | |
| | Hung, A. H. | Pte., R.M. (P) | |
| PO 8240 | Hobbs, W. | | |
| RMA 5448 | Hewitt, G. E. | | |
| RMA 5293 | Hickling, J. S. | | |
| PO 8964 | Hussey, A. B. | | |
| PO 8906 | Hawes, G. H. | | |
| 170306 | Ingroville, T. P. | Captain, R.N. (P) | |
| 286376 | Ivory, J, O'D. | Mid. | |
| PO 8878 | Ivery, G. | Mid. | |
| | | Major R.M.L.I. (P) | |
| | Jellicoe, J. R. | A.B. | |
| | Jones, W. B. C. | P.O. 2nd Class | |
| | Jermain, R. L. | A.B. | |
| | Johnstone, J. R. | A.B. | |
| 176171 | Johnson, W. | 2nd Yeo. Sigs. (P) | |
| 169533 | Joyce, W. E. | A.B. | |
| 160124 | Jordan, P. J. M. | Stoker | |
| 166373 | Johnson, T. A. | Gunner R.M.A. (P) | |
| 182802 | Jago, F. | Gunner R.M.A. | |
| 190268 | Jackson, H. L. | Gunner R.M.A. | |
| 173932 | Jordan, J. J. | Dom. 2nd Class | |
| 282128 | Jeffery, F. G. | | |
| RMA 5665 | Jupp, W. H. | | |
| RMA 5930 | James, G. D. | | |
| RMA 5999 | Johnson, H. R. | | |
| | Jing, T. W. | | |
| 149668 | Keegan, A. J. | A.B. | |
| 188336 | Kimber, J. H. N. | A.B. | |
| 186346 | King, F. | Gunner R.M.A. | |
| RMA 4562 | Kemp, G. | Pte., R.M. | |
| PO 6974 | Kippen, C. | Gunner R.M.A. | |
| RMA 3687 | King, A. | Pte., R.M. | |
| PLY 9126 | Knowles, C. | | |
| | Littlejohns, W. G. | Asst. Paymaster (P) | |
| | Luttrell, J. L. F. | Lieut. (P) | |
| | Lower-Crofton, E. G. | Lieut. | |

35

| Number | Name | Rating |
|---|---|---|
| 157596 | Lewis, A. M. | A.B. |
| 129130 | Legg, W. | P.O. 1st Class |
| 182455 | Lockyer, W. J. | A.B. |
| 183633 | Livermore, A. G. N. | Ldg. Seaman (P) |
| 190614 | Lloyd, W. T. | Ord. |
| 140074 | Long, E. J. | A.B. |
|  | Loy, A. H. | Dom. 3rd Class |
| PO 7799 | Lambert, C. | Pte., R.M. |
| PO 1494 | Lawrence, H. J. | Sgt., R.M. |
| PO 3846 | Lepine, R. J. | Pte., R.M. (P) |
| PO 7272 | Louch, H. W. | Pte., R.M. |
| PO 8247 | Lawson, L. A. | Pte., R.M. |
| 182941 | Manistry, H. W. E. | Asst. Paymaster |
| 157414 | Morgan, W. | A.B. (D) |
| 151904 | Moore, W. | Ldg. Seaman (P) |
| 186414 | McElligott, M. | P.O. 1st Class (P) |
| 186415 | McKee, G. | A.B. |
| 166381 | McBride, J. | A.B. (D) |
| 186700 | Morgan, H. | A.B. |
| 142846 | Mintram, A. S. | A.B. (P) |
| 197902 | Madge, L. J. H. | P.O. 1st Class (P) |
| 196369 | Mercer, E. | Ord. |
| 282122 | Melbourne, H. | Ord. |
| 286732 | Mills, J. C. | Stoker (P) |
| 286375 | Mulcahy, E. | Stoker (P) |
| 131777 | McAulay, W. | Stoker |
| 341351 | Maze, D. E. | C.E.R.A. 2nd Class |
| 350416 | McGeorge, J. W. | Ldg. Shipwright (P) |
| 350336 | Moull, W. D. | 2nd S.B. Steward (P) |
|  | McLean, W. G. | S.S. Asst. (P) |
| RMA 5718 | Martin, H. | Gunner R.M.A. |
| RMA 5239 | Marden, W. | Gunner R.M.A. |
| RMA 3413 | Miller, H. C. | Lance Sgt. (P) |
| PO 9034 | McKenzie, J. | Pte., R.M. (P) |
| PO 6163 | Metcalf, C. H. | Lance Corp. (P) |
| 189313 | Neil, W. | A.B. |
| 183348 | Newman, S. G. | A.B. |
| 187722 | Negus, C. H. | A.B. |
| 192921 | Neale, H. J. | A.B. (D) |
| 282147 | Newton, J. | Stoker |
| 171194 | Nichols, S. | Stoker |
| 281536 | Newman, A. J. | Stoker |
| RMA 5754 | Neilson, J. | Gunner R.M.A. |
| PO 8036 | Nicholson, W. A. | Pte., R.M. |
|  | Osborne, E. O. B. S. | Mid. |
| 185897 | Outram, C. | A.B. |
|  | Powlett, F. A. | Flag Lieutenant |
|  | Pickthorn, E. B. | Staff Surgeon (P) |
| 180912 | Pearton, W. J. | A.B. |
| 186391 | Povey, G. | A.B. |
| 109455 | Pitman, A. E. | A.B. |
| 149951 | Penn, W. | P.O. 1st Class |
| 112574 | Pond, C. H. | A.B. |
| 193464 | Pay, J. R. | Ord. |
| 189165 | Paskins, T. F. | A.B. |
| 183754 | Purnell, E. O. | Stoker (DD) |
| 170229 | Parsons, A. | Stoker |
| 286362 | Prior, G. W. C. | Stoker |
| 281631 | Phillips, W. | Stoker |
| 120468 | Poulter, E. R. | Ship's Corp. 1st Class |
| 350119 | Parry, F. G. | Bugler, R.M. (D) |
| PO 6711 | Priscott, A. | Gunner, R.M.A. |
| RMA 6774 | Pook, E. R. | Pte., R.M. |
| PLY 8603 | Pearman, H. E. | Pte., R.M. |
|  | Riley, E. W. | Asst. Engineer |
|  | Rotter, C. J. E. | Paymaster |
| 123562 | Regis, H. W. | Yeo. Sig. (P) |
| 118704 | Read, J. | A.B. |
| 151659 | Restall, T. J. | Ldg. Seaman |
| 118046 | Richards, R. C. | A.B. |
| 179283 | Reeve, A. D. | A.B. (P) |
| 157415 | Rogers, W. H. | P.O. 2nd Class |
| 185669 | Reed, F. | A.B. |
| 188625 | Reeves, G. J. | A.B. |
| 184708 | Reeves, J. | A.B. |
| 185810 | Richardson, G. P. | A.B. |
| 173913 | Roberts, A. E. | A.B. |
| 170038 | Richardson, J. | Ldg. Seaman |
| 341124 | Robinson, A. E. | Blacksmith's Mate (D) |

| Number | Name | Rating |
|---|---|---|
| PO 3695 | Read, T. B. | Pte., R.M. |
| RMA 4240 | Rann, W. H. | Cook's Mate |
| RMA 6409 | Russell, F. | |
| 160642 | Rodden, C. | |
| | Seymour, Sir E. H. | Vice-Admiral (P) |
| | Smith, Rev. E. F. H. | Chaplain and Naval Instructor |
| | Sinclair, C. H. | Lieutenant |
| | Starr, G. H. | Asst. Engineer |
| | Sibbald, T. M. | Fleet Surgeon (DD) |
| | St. John, S. E. A. O. | Mid. (3. Ds) |
| | Shephard, H. L. | Act. Gunner |
| | Sammels, F. E. | |
| 152858 | Sullivan, J. | P.O. 2nd Class |
| 182968 | Sanderson, J. E. | A.B. |
| 143729 | Skipsey, R. | A.B. |
| 171503 | Smyth, D. W. | P.O. 1st Class (P) |
| 124233 | Spiller, G. | P.O. 1st Class |
| 148266 | Small, A. | Ldg. Seaman (P) |
| 150755 | Silvester, J. | P.O. 2nd Class |
| 121844 | Spencer, A. | A.B. |
| 184348 | Sasse, A. J. | A.B. |
| 184293 | Shepherd, W. J. | A.B. |
| 185799 | Sippets, G. | A.B. |
| 121405 | Shilston, A. E. | P.O. 1st Class (P) |
| 184008 | Spratley, A. | A.B. |
| 190281 | Sawkings, E. J. | Ord. (D) |
| 191864 | Smith, J. A. | A.B. |
| 188893 | Sharpe, F. | P.O. 2nd Class |
| 137166 | Samphier, H. | A.B. (P) |
| 189160 | Swiggs, A. E. | Stoker |
| 111634 | Shailer, T. P. | Stoker |
| 292073 | Smith, G. | Armourer (P) |
| 129367 | Solen, J. T. | Pte., R.M. |
| PO 4379 | Stainfield, A. F. J. | Pte., R.M. |
| PO 8252 | Smith, W. J. | Gunner, R.M.A. |
| RMA 4466 | Stevens, R. | Gunner, R.M.A. |
| RMA 5851 | Simpson, E. J. | Pte., R.M. |
| PO 6748 | Summerton, H. | Pte., R.M. |
| PO 5040 | Smith, F. | Pte., R.M. (P) |
| PLY 4983 | Stimpson, H. | Gunner, R.M.A. |
| RMA 4294 | | |
| CH 8612 | Searle, J. | Pte., R.M. |
| 340949 | Stanberg, E. | Clerk |
| | Tabuteau, A. E. | Dom. 1st Class |
| 174826 | Tai, A. H. | A.B. |
| 156075 | Townsend, T. | P.O. 1st Class |
| 151105 | Tooze, S. J. S. | P.O. 2nd Class |
| 123861 | Tripp, R. | A.B. |
| 179709 | Tagg, G. W. | A.B. |
| 185898 | Temple, G. H. | A.B. |
| 157604 | Taylor, F. | A.B. |
| 179102 | Tulett, J. | P.O. 1st Class |
| 149558 | Turner, E. | Ldg. Stoker 1st Class |
| 280718 | Torrington, B. | Stoker |
| 268357 | Towner, F. H. W. | E.R.A. 3rd Class |
| 282730 | Thompson, W. | Stoker |
| 280748 | Toal, J. | Stoker |
| 176043 | Townsend, J. T. | Stoker |
| PO 7625 | Thompson, A. C. | Lance Sgt., R.M. |
| RMA 5771 | Trodd, H. M. | Gunner, R.M.A. |
| | Tanner, J. F. | |
| 165150 | Vine, W. G. | P.O. 2nd Class (P) |
| 286596 | Venton, L. | Stoker (P) |
| | Wilson, F. O'B. | Mid. |
| | Wan, A. H. | Dom. 1st Class |
| 104052 | Wyatt, E. S. | C.P.O. |
| | Wah, A. H. | Dom. 1st Class |
| | Wing, Ching | Dom. 1st Class |
| 123957 | Webber, F. A. | Dom. 1st Class (P) |
| 183260 | Williams, G. | A.B. |
| 183479 | Whatley, F. | A.B. |
| 128620 | Webber, E. | P.O. 1st Class |
| 139993 | Wilson, W. | Ldg. Seaman |
| 165392 | Wardner, E. C. | A.B. |
| 137409 | Whitecross, P. A. | A.B. (P) |
| 102529 | Whaley, W. | P.O. 1st Class |
| 147436 | Whyte, C. L. C. B. | P.O. 2nd Class |
| 161349 | Wright, T. | Ldg. Seaman |
| 188619 | Walker, J. | A.B. |
| 186986 | Wilkinson, W. | A.B. |

37

| | | |
|---|---|---|
| 159070 | Wildbore, R. F. | A.B. |
| 186305 | Welch, G. W. | A.B. |
| 183912 | Wilson, W. | Ord. |
| 146145 | Woodriffe, S. C. | Ord. |
| 160836 | Willis, J. C. | P.O. 1st Class |
| 282983 | Wilkinson, F. W. | Ldg. Seaman |
| 286052 | Waters, J. | Stoker |
| 286521 | Waghorn, B. B. | Stoker (D) |
| 280253 | Walker, E. | Stoker (D) |
| RMA 4267 | Willcox, O. H. | Stoker |
| RMA 6102 | Walker, W. G. | Gunner, R.M.A. (P) |
| CH 8975 | West, F. | Gunner, R:M.A. |
| RMA 5415 | Weston, E. | Pte., R.M. |
| | | Gunner, R.M.A. |
| 286622 | Young, M. | Stoker (P) |
| | Ying, A. H. | Dom. 3rd Class |
| RMA 5890 | Yates, J. T. | Gunner, R.M.A. (DD) |

## HMS *Endymion*

| | | |
|---|---|---|
| 123194 | Akehurst, E. J. | P.O. 1st Class |
| 197136 | Avent, W. S. | A.B. |
| 194098 | Adkins, C. A. | A.B. |
| 289648 | Adams, D. | Stoker |
| PO 9560 | Arnold, A. W. | Pte., R.M. |
| PO 8530 | Ash, F. T. | Pte., R.M. |
| PO 8718 | Austin, J. T. | Pte., R.M. |
| | Boothby, W. O. | Commander, R.N. |
| | Braithwaite, L. W. | Sub-Lieutenant |
| | Brownrigg, H. J. S. | Mid. |
| 160890 | Banfield, A. | Ldg. Seaman |
| 157937 | Buzyacott, R. W. | A.B. |
| 197093 | Burgess, F. | Ord. |
| 190190 | Bailey, J. | Ord. |
| 149657 | Baldock, W. | P.O. 1st Class |
| 156091 | Bartlett, E. C. | A.B. |
| 163394 | Billett, J. W. | A.B. |
| 148885 | Butt, J. | A.B. |
| 192173 | Bleach, R. H. | Ord. |
| 200787 | Buckley, J. | Ord. |
| 189357 | | A.B. |
| 188877 | Boxwell, F. G. | A.B. |
| 184604 | Briard, F. W. | A.B. |
| 194393 | Brooker, H. | Ord. |
| 192870 | Brander, J. A. | Ord. |
| 192846 | Bowhey, A. H. | Ord. |
| 194983 | Burrows, W. J. | A.B. |
| 184170 | Barlow, A. W. | Stoker |
| 276722 | Buck, P. | Stoker |
| 284789 | Barnard, G. | Stoker |
| 135609 | Batchelder, J. S. | S.B.S. |
| 140886 | Buttonshaw, H. F. | Pte., R.M. |
| PO 6091 | Bell, J. G. | Corp., R.M. |
| PO 7718 | Baker, C. W. G. | Lance Corp. |
| PO 8943 | Bradley, J. L. | Pte., R.M. |
| PO 9571 | Bristow, R. | Pte., R.M. |
| PO 9573 | Barton, R. | Pte., R.M. |
| PO 7101 | Bartlett, T. C. | |
| 112358 | Colomb, H. W. | Lieut., R.N. |
| 129795 | Callaghan, G. A. | Captain, R.N. |
| 167872 | Crichton, C. L. M. | Mid. |
| 152172 | Conway, C. E. | C.P.O. |
| 196447 | Charles, G. W. | P.O. 1st Class |
| 190138 | Carter, A. J. | P.O. 2nd Class |
| 151057 | Charlo, H. | P.O. 1st Class |
| 144284 | Chesnutt, T. | Ord. |
| 144161 | Cole, G. | P.O. 2nd Class |
| 162953 | Cowell, R. A. | A.B. |
| 171119 | Clancy, M. | A.B. |
| 193209 | Connolly, A. | A.B. |
| 168391 | Carr, R. | A.B. |
| 188962 | Crow, A. G. | A.B. |
| 192135 | Cavan, S. | A.B. (D) |
| 175327 | Cater, H. | A.B. |
| 191750 | Catchpole, J. | A.B. |
| 155628 | Carraher, M. | Ord. |
| 169050 | Clarke, J. C. | 2nd Yeo. Sig. |
| 280189 | Curtis, J. E. | Ldg. Stoker 1st Class |
| 289667 | Combs, J. | Stoker |
| | Cheeseman, A. | Stoker |
| | Clark, W. | |
| | Cox, W. H. | |

38

| | | | |
|---|---|---|---|
| 287549 | Coleman, W. | | Stoker |
| 117789 | Craggs, E. E. | | Armourer's Crew |
| PO 8688 | Constable, J. W. D. | | Bugler, R.M. |
| PO 9563 | Chapman, F. J. | | Pte., R.M. |
| PO 8806 | Cartwright, W. A. | | Pte., R.M. (D) |
| CH 9131 | Chandler, W. | | Pte., R.M. |
| | | | |
| 164380 | Doig, R. O. M. | | Captain, R.M.L.I. |
| 165054 | Davey, A. C. | | P.O. 1st Class |
| 164345 | Dickinson, J. H. | | P.O. 2nd Class |
| 287519 | Dummer, S. | | A.B. |
| 280338 | Denyer, R. | | Stoker (D) |
| PO 9572 | Day, J. | | Stoker |
| PO 8760 | Dryman, A. | | Pte., R.M. |
| | Day, G. | | Pte., R.M. |
| | | | |
| 183655 | Ealey, J. | | Ord. |
| 195230 | Edgington, C. | | Ord. |
| PO 8145 | Edwards, G. J. E. | | Pte., R.M. |
| PO 8976 | Eastman, G. | | Pte., R.M. (D) |
| PO 9068 | Ewens, S. | | Pte., R.M. |
| | | | |
| 166037 | Frith, E. O. | | P.O. 1st Class |
| 118530 | Ford, H. | | P.O. 1st Class |
| 147621 | Flory, W. | | A.B. (DD) |
| 197743 | Flory, W. J. | | Ord. |
| 185677 | Francis, A. G. | | A.B. |
| 192781 | Fluellen, H. W. | | Ord. |
| 195635 | Flack, H. H. | | Ord. |
| 158342 | Facey, A. J. | | Stoker |
| | | | |
| 190184 | Gill, R. P. J. | | Ord. |
| 162824 | Goubert, E. J. | | Ldg. Seaman |
| 178500 | Guerin, P. | | A.B. (D) |
| 178736 | Golding, W. H. | | A.B. |
| 190613 | Griffiths, H. G. | | Ord. |
| 195637 | Grapham, W. A. | | Ord. |
| 195380 | Gussin, G. H. | | Ord. (D) |
| 151559 | Gaskin, R. H. | | Yeo. Sig. |
| 167191 | Green, A. | | Stoker (D) |
| 283017 | Graves, W. J. H. | | Stoker |
| 276140 | Gray, A. | | Ldg. Stoker 2nd Class (D) |
| | | | |
| 175972 | Gould, J. | | Stoker |
| 163611 | Goodman, F. | | Carpenter's Mate |
| 124049 | Grose, J. W. | | Armourer |
| | Gun, A. | | Dom. 2nd Class |
| PO 9554 | Gill, S. | | Pte., R.M. |
| PO 2311 | Govin, J. | | Pte., R.M. |
| CH 6793 | Galliford, J. T. | | Lance Sgt., R.M. (P) |
| | | | |
| 197016 | Hewitt, B. L. | | Mid. |
| 197843 | Homan, E. A. | | Mid. |
| 197054 | Holder, S. E. | | Mid. |
| 198108 | Hanna, J. | | Ord. |
| 197857 | Hodgers, M. | | Ord. (D) |
| 156375 | Hurrell, H. G. | | Ord. |
| 143045 | Holmes, J. | | Ord. |
| 197813 | Hodges, N. | | A.B. |
| 191375 | Hardy, J. H. | | A.B. |
| 192282 | Hurren, J. | | Ord. |
| 191456 | Hargadon, J. | | A.B. |
| 194177 | Hatton, J. D. | | Ord. (D) |
| 195376 | Hallett, W. P. | | Ord. |
| 286725 | Hartnett, E. | | Ord. (D) |
| 288686 | Henry, W. S. | | Stoker |
| 289656 | Hall, G. | | Stoker (D) |
| 340670 | Hazlehurst, J. | | Stoker |
| 350425 | Hamilton, F. | | Plumber |
| PO 2375 | Harvey, G. F. | | S.B.A. |
| PO 4539 | Holland, H. A. | | Pte., R.M. |
| PO 9579 | Hayward, G. | | Pte., R.M. |
| PO 9553 | Hann, F. | | Pte., R.M. |
| PO 9323 | Howse, C. A. | | Corp., R.M. |
| PO 6445 | Hayes, S. J. | | Pte., R.M. |
| PO 8771 | Hutchinson, D. | | Pte., R.M. |
| | Herrick, H. | | |
| | Hutchins, W. G. | | |

39

| | | |
|---|---|---|
| 148091 | Isaac, J. H. | P.O. 1st Class |
| 139105 | Jones, P. S. | A.B. |
| 169432 | Jones, E. | Ldg. Seaman |
| 193016 | James, T. | Ord. |
| 192606 | Jones, J. | Ord. |
| 289233 | Joyce, T. | Stoker |
| PO 8209 | Jones, A. | Pte., R.M. |
| PO 8740 | Jones, W. | Pte., R.M. (D) |
| 175557 | Kirkham, W. C. | Ldg. Seaman |
| 163023 | Knight, G. H. | A.B. |
| 196771 | Kinch, G. H. | Ord. |
| 169059 | Kite, H. | Stoker |
| 135259 | Kelsey, G. W. | Armourer |
| PO 9566 | King, W. J. | Pte., R.M. |
| 151798 | Leishman, J. C. | Chaplain |
| 182693 | Luker, W. | P.O. 1st Class |
| 158149 | Lewis, W. | A.B. |
| 171390 | Leggett, A. S. | A.B. |
| 163613 | Lawrence, H. A. | Ldg. Sig. |
| 341362 | Legg, G. | Ldg. Shipwright |
| 340880 | Luck, G. E. R. | Armourer's Crew |
| PO 9390 | Liddell, H. | Cook's Mate |
| PO 9558 | Lock, C. J. | Pte., R.M. |
| PO 9567 | Logan, W. | Pte., R.M. |
| PO 8823 | Lower, H. | Pte., R.M. |
| | Louge, W. A. | Pte., R.M. |
| | McGachen, F. S. | Mid. |
| | McClure, H. R. | Mid. |
| | MacNamara, E. D. | Surgeon |
| 171157 | Martin, J. C. | Ldg. Seaman |
| 143856 | Murphy, D. | Ldg. Seaman |
| 197844 | Murphy, R. | Ord. |
| 170362 | Mitchell, G. J. | A.B. |
| 173166 | Moore, M. | A.B. (D) |
| 192926 | Mann, G. | Ord. |
| 193936 | Mansbridge, J. | A.B. |
| 195236 | McDermott, J. | A.B. (D) |
| 192445 | Martin, A. E. | Ord. |
| 196477 | Morris, M. | Ord. |
| 195634 | Mills, G. R. | Qtk. Sig. |
| 191274 | Merritt, C. W. | Stoker |
| 285199 | Mesor C. | Stoker |
| 285206 | McIntosh, D. | Shipwright |
| 342702 | Montgomery, J. W. | Corp., R.M. |
| PO 5936 | Moore, G. F. | Pte., R.M. |
| PO 9575 | Marchant, W. | |
| 139206 | Newman, H. C. | P.O. 1st Class |
| 193431 | Nethercott, C. | Ord. |
| 280877 | Newlove, G. | Stoker |
| 289225 | Northover, F. | Stoker |
| PO 8952 | Neighbour, A. E. | Pte., R.M. |
| 192599 | Osborne, F. | Ord. |
| CH 11613 | Owen, A. | Pte., R.M. |
| PO 9564 | Oake, A. A. J. R. | Pte., R.M. |
| CH 7612 | Oakley, J. | Lance Corp., R.M. |
| 196804 | Powell, F. | Lieut., R.M. |
| 197183 | Popplestone, E. D. | Ord. |
| 124694 | Pym, F. E. | A.B. |
| 125051 | Pask, W. | A.B. |
| 159665 | Phillips, A. F. | A.B. |
| 190070 | Perrin, R. H. | Ord. |
| 194972 | Price, W. | Ord. |
| 195630 | Pearson, J. | Bugler |
| PO 8441 | Parsons, G. | Pte., R.M. |
| PO 8321 | Parker, C. W. | Pte., R.M. |
| PO 9565 | Phillips, J. W. | Pte., R.M. |
| PO 8729 | Parker, J. J. | Pte., R.M. |
| PO 8820 | Pink, J. | Pte., R.M. |
| PO 95174 | Philpot, W. | Pte., R.M. |
| | Price, A. | |
| PO 7958 | Quaife, A. | Pte., R.M. |
| | Robinson, E. G. | Mid. |
| 140249 | Rowsell, D. W. | A.B. |

| | | | |
|---|---|---|---|
| 195969 | Reddan, P. | A.B. (D) | |
| 196445 | Randells, C. | Ord. | |
| 162216 | Richards, F. G. | Ldg. Seaman | |
| 193310 | Roskelly, J. A. | Ord. | |
| 187069 | Russell, F. R. | Ord. | |
| 183837 | Rixon, F. | A.B. | |
| 192893 | Rennell, W. J. | Ord. | |
| 192064 | Read, W. J. | Ord. (D) | |
| 192647 | Ross, A. | Ord. | |
| 174567 | Rimmer, C. | Qdk. Sig. (D) | |
| 192516 | Redwood, A. | Ord. | |
| 281707 | Rhimes, R. | Stoker | |
| PO 6819 | Rogers, A. J. | Corp., R.M. | |
| PO 5117 | Reynolds, E. G. | Pte., R.M. | |
| PO 9556 | Ravenall, W. G. | Pte., R.M. | |
| PO 8766 | Richards, W. | Pte., R.M. | |
| | | | |
| 156111 | Silk, E. S. | Engineer | |
| 196481 | Shanahan, F. | P.O. 2nd Class | |
| 112182 | Simpson, T. | Ord. | |
| 192300 | Soper, J. | A.B. | |
| 191049 | Start, G. | A.B. | |
| 165132 | Smith, W. | Ord. | |
| 161508 | Symes, F. | Ldg. Seaman | |
| 194569 | Sweet, G. E. | A.B. | |
| 195354 | Saunders, A. E. | Ord. | |
| 192842 | Speight, B. | Ord. | |
| 195642 | Smale, R. G. A. | Ord. | |
| 146126 | Scanlon, E. E. | Stoker | |
| 287054 | Seager, J. | Stoker | |
| 166261 | Smith, J. | 2nd Wtr. | |
| PO 8743 | Smith, J. | Pte., R.M. | |
| PO 9438 | Strachan, A. | Pte., R.M. (D) | |
| PO 9447 | Semple, A. | Pte., R.M. | |
| PO 9578 | Smith, W. | Pte., R.M. | |
| PO 8813 | Sanctuary, G. W. | Pte., R.M. | |
| PLY 7749 | Smart, J. | Pte., R.M. | |
| | Stanford, W. | Pte., R.M. | |
| | | | |
| | Thurstan, N. M. | Mid. | |
| | Thomas, J. L. | Fleet Surgeon | |
| | Tier, L. E. | Asst. Paymaster (D) | |
| 121592 | Thompson, A. | P.O. 1st Class | |
| 167843 | Tomkin, W. E. | P.O. 2nd Class | |
| 196493 | Tyrell, W. | Ord. | |
| 177024 | Towton, T. F. | A.B. | |
| 194786 | Templeman, E. J. | Sig. | |
| 195629 | Tucker, E. C. | Ord. | |
| 269208 | Taylor, W. | E.R.A. 4th Class | |
| PO 9370 | Thornton, J. H. | Pte., R.M. | |
| | | | |
| 188181 | Usmar, B. | A.B. | |
| | | | |
| 188689 | Vinicombe, G. W. | A.B. | |
| PO 9581 | Vince, J. J. | Pte., R.M. | |
| | | | |
| 139778 | Wooldridge, S. E. | P.O. 1st Class (DD) | |
| 147313 | Walker, G. | A.B. | |
| 176487 | Wilkins, R. J. | Ldg. Seaman | |
| 190756 | Wilcox, W. | A.B. | |
| 144632 | Williams, E. | A.B. | |
| 167503 | Wright, R. | A.B. | |
| 192403 | Watson, D. | Ord. | |
| 190155 | Wyer, J. | Ord. | |
| 195623 | Woolacott, H. J. | Ord. | |
| 194545 | Walsh, T. | Ord. | |
| 194761 | Wooledge, W. C. | Ord. | |
| 195201 | Walker, P. | Ord. | |
| 194916 | Weller, J. H. | Ldg. Stoker 1st Class | |
| 279557 | Wooley, T. | Stoker | |
| 289658 | Woodward, W. T. | Ship's Corp. 1st Class | |
| 139826 | Widdicombe, W. H. | Dom. 2nd Class | |
| | Woo, A. H. | Pte., R.M. (D) | |
| PO 9550 | Williams, A. H. | Pte., R.M. | |
| PO 9551 | Windsor, A. H. | Pte., R.M. | |
| PO 5481 | Wright, J. B. | | |
| | | | |
| 192941 | Yates, B. C. | Ord. | |
| 289623 | Yates, J. | Stoker | |

# HMS *Orlando*

| | | |
|---|---|---|
| 161550 | Aymer, F. | Bandsman |
| 288978 | Allen, W. B. | Sgt., R.M. |
| 158970 | Allen, G. W. | Pte., R.M. |
| 147456 | Burke, F. H. T. | Mid. |
| 140038 | Buttrick, W. | A.B. |
| 147106 | Bailey, G. F. | A.B. |
| 177875 | Bicknell, D. | A.B. |
| 170653 | Bisson, P. E. | A.B. (D) |
| 185707 | Bingham, W. | A.B. |
| 194694 | Bocock, F. T. | A.B. (D) |
| 197904 | Berrecloth, W. J. | A.B. |
| 185726 | Berry, H. | |
| 184599 | Barge, L. | P.O. 1st Class |
| 177041 | Brogan, E. A. | A.B. |
| 161247 | Burnicle, R. | P.O. 1st Class |
| 151534 | Barnes, W. | Stoker (D) |
| 340888 | Bennett, J. W. | Stoker |
| 340634 | Betts, W. | Shipwright |
| | Blyth, R. | Bugler (P) |
| 152818 | Collett, J. A. | Lieut., R.N. |
| 143745 | Carter, R. H. | A.B. (D) |
| 172363 | Cooper, A. | A.B. |
| 180148 | Cummings, B. J. | |
| 186540 | Cunningham, H. C. T. | Lieut., R.N. |
| 183203 | Campion, H. C. T. | Mid. (P) |
| 194251 | Cunningham, J. E. | P.O. 1st Class |
| 129796 | Cranston, A. G. | P.O. 2nd Class |
| 147000 | Curchod, C. S. | A.B. |
| 171400 | Cox, C. R. | A.B. |
| 182153 | Chapman, J. H. | Ldg. Seaman (P) |
| 190788 | Cole, E. | Ldg. Sig. |
| 193819 | Cook, J. F. | A.B. |
| 268296 | Clark, A. V. | Stoker |
| 288963 | Craddock, E. H. | Stoker |
| 340579 | Catton, W. H. | Stoker |
| 340737 | Clarke, A. E. | Stoker |
| | Chapman, A. W. | Sgt., R.M. |
| | Curd, B. | |

| | | |
|---|---|---|
| 357147 | Crout, J. | |
| PO, 5593 | Carpenter R. J. | |
| PO, 9114 | Cook F. W. | |
| | Dumaresq, C. P. | |
| 173468 | Drew, C. H. | |
| 177955 | Duke, F. G. | |
| 160129 | Drake, A. | |
| 171583 | Davidson, T. H. | |
| 170316 | Donovan, T. | |
| 188878 | Dunleavy, J. | |
| 193525 | Dines, J. | |
| 191840 | Durham, J. | |
| 180161 | Daily, J. | |
| 139733 | Ellis, J. H. | |
| 171613 | Easman, F. G. | |
| 157785 | Eyles, H. | |
| 279781 | Edwards, J. W. | |
| 279794 | Elliot, W. | |
| 342457 | Edwards, J. W. | |
| PO 8657 | Ettie, O. R. B. | |
| 171632 | Fisher, F. C. | |
| 183531 | Fitz, H. P. | |
| | Foot, R. G. | |
| | Garforth, F. E. M. | |
| 87954 | Gipps, G. | |
| | Giles, H. | |
| 161502 | Gamblen, H. V. | |
| 175495 | Goble, A. T. | |
| 187895 | Grigg, C. | |
| 162772 | George, H. E. | |
| 184704 | Gaion, S. | |
| 194653 | Glew, J. | |
| 285276 | Gates, C. | |
| 276417 | Godfrey, W. J. | |
| 280017 | Gaskin, W. R. | |
| 290942 | Griffin, P. | |
| PLY 3769 | Gingell, W. | |

42

| Number | Name | Rank |
|---|---|---|
| 129175 | Hunt, F. F. | P.O. 1st Class |
| 149616 | Hicks, H. R. | P.O. 2nd Class |
| 158460 | Hood, F. G. K. | A.B. |
| 169386 | Higgins, T. E. | A.B. |
| 178735 | Hussey, F. J. | Ldg. Seaman |
| 147697 | Hinton, F. | A.B. |
| 179715 | Hoddell, W. | A.B. |
| 186657 | Hibberd, A. E. | Ord. |
| 195558 | Hawkins, B. R. | A.B. |
| 192751 | Hanson, L. | A.B. |
| 189191 | Hood, A. | Stoker |
| 283691 | Hutton, A. F. | Stoker |
| 288981 | Howard, T. | Lance Sgt., R.M. |
| PO 5588 | Hicks, T. G. | Pte., R.M. |
| PO 9246 | Hodgkins, J. H. | Pte., R.M. |
| PO 9254 | Hewitt, J. | Chief Stoker |
| 162097 | Irish, H. | |
| 354902 | Jefferson, H. | Lieut., R.N. |
| PO 9249 | Johnson, J. | Stoker |
| PO 9276 | Johnson, F. A. | Pte., R.M. |
| | Jones, F. T. | Lance Corp., R.M. |
| 183532 | Kelling, W. C. | A.B. |
| 194111 | Keeling, J. E. | Ord. |
| PO 9242 | King, C. E. | Pte., R.M. |
| 278544 | Littledale, H. F. | Mid. |
| PO 9343 | Lee, J. R. | Stoker |
| PO 5395 | Lewis, A. | Pte., R.M. |
| | Lye, A. H. T. | Corp., R.M. |
| 160158 | Murray, E. F. | Asst. Paymaster |
| 176241 | McGuire, P. | Gunner |
| 179839 | Mowatt, W. H. | Ldg. Seaman |
| 191041 | Mills, W. | A.B. |
| 184324 | Mills, H. T. | A.B. |
| 188006 | Merwood, F. G. | A.B. |
| 193256 | Mosley, R. G. | A.B. |
| 158581 | Mason, E. J. | A.B. |
| | McCarthy, M. | A.B. |
| | Mulford, B. | Ldg. Stoker 1st Class |
| 282207 | Milroy, W. G. | Stoker |
| 281335 | Murrell, W. | Stoker |
| 279762 | Molyneux, J. | Stoker (D) |
| 288492 | McDonald, J. | Stoker |
| 288516 | McIlhone, C. | Stoker |
| 131768 | Moore, J. | Carp's. Mate |
| 341020 | Meade, W. E. | S.St. Assit. |
| PO 6918 | Marr, J. E. | Pte., R.M. (D) |
| PO 9250 | Morley, W. | Pte., R.M. |
| 169038 | Norman, W. C. | A.B. |
| 191343 | North, G. | A.B. |
| 142224 | New, C. H. | Ldg. Seaman |
| PO 9240 | Newcombe, H. J. | Pte., R.M. (D) |
| 191136 | Oats, W. J. | Ord. (D) |
| 113832 | Polhill, T. | P.O. 1st Class |
| 86245 | Padbury, W. F. | P.O. 1st Class |
| 193207 | Parr, W. | A.B. |
| 153356 | Picot, G. P. | A.B. |
| 179091 | Purchess, J. | A.B. |
| 190000 | Palmer, F. A. | A.B. |
| 152284 | Penney, G. E. | A.B. |
| 147713 | Payne, T. C. | A.B. |
| 191341 | Parsons, L. V. | Ord. |
| 194109 | Perry, W. H. | A.B. |
| 194337 | Pope, W. J. | A.B. |
| 288549 | Parsons, J. H. | Stoker |
| 288962 | Parker, W. J. | Stoker |
| 288272 | Plant, W. J. | Stoker (D) |
| 340806 | Phillips, P. | Bandsman |
| PO 7459 | Page, J. | Pte., R.M. |
| 109054 | Robinson, C. V. | Mid. |
| 185409 | Roberts, F. W. | P.O. 1st Class |
| 191851 | Rees, J. H. | A.B. |
| 283792 | Robinson, G. | A.B. (D) |
| 340910 | Rowney, J. H. | Stoker |
| 340333 | Robbins, A. H. | Ldg. Shipwright |
| | Reynolds, G. L. | Bandsman |
| PO9292 | Robinson, E. J. | Pte., R.M. |

| | | |
|---|---|---|
| PO 9142 | Ransom, T. | Pte., R.M. |
| Po 8934 | Robinson, H. | Pte., R.M. |
| | | |
| 192826 | Stanley, E. A. B. | Mid. |
| 184269 | Spencer, F. | Ord. |
| 153532 | Snelgrove, W. | A.B. |
| 173324 | Samways, G. | A.B. |
| 184327 | Symes, T. | A.B. |
| 196208 | Sturgess, H. | A.B. |
| 195886 | Smith, R. | Ord. |
| 185724 | Shea, J. | Sig. |
| 291789 | Staples, E. C. | Stoker |
| PO 8874 | Searls, P. | Pte., R.M. |
| | Stillwell, H. G. | |
| | | |
| 126498 | Taylor, G. W. | Mid. |
| 177774 | Thomas, H. | P.O. 1st Class |
| 165167 | Taplin, W. | A.B. |
| 128091 | Tyler, A. J. G. | A.B. |
| 179987 | Taylor, W. J. | Ldg. Seaman |
| 184815 | Tubb, J. V. | A.B. |
| 340069 | Tuck, T. | Cooper's crew |
| PO 9241 | Thomson, D. E. | Pte., R.M. |
| | Taylor, A. | |
| | | |
| 125874 | Wright, P. N. | Commander |
| 107642 | Whiteing, C. A. | P.O. 1st Class |
| 162314 | White, W. F. | P.O. 1st Class |
| 162456 | Whitmore, A. | A.B. |
| 176425 | Walker, J. E. | A.B. |
| 170663 | Weippert, A. E. | A.B. |
| 179036 | Woolfries, H. W. | A.B. |
| 117015 | Wedge, A. G. | A.B. |
| 188651 | Wellard, H. R. | A.B. |
| 182758 | Wheeler, R. G. | A.B. |
| 184785 | Willcox, T. | Ord. |
| 192617 | Wills, T. W. | Ord. |
| 192030 | Wilson, W. | A.B. |
| | West, G. H. | |

## Naval Depot Wei Hai Wei

| | | |
|---|---|---|
| CH 4888 | Adcock, A. | Bugler |
| CH 9539 | Anderson, J. | Pte., R.M. |
| PLY 4974 | Atkins, J. E. | Pte., R.M. |
| CH 9571 | Adams, A. | Pte., R.M. |
| PLY 8604 | Adams, J. | Pte., R.M. |
| PLY 8615 | Andrews, A. | Pte., R.M. |
| | | |
| PO 1080 | Boyle, J. | Pte., R.M. |
| PLY 8619 | Brooks, B. | Pte., R.M. |
| CH 9895 | Ball, J. W. | Pte., R.M. |
| CH 8882 | Bell, C. R. | Pte., R.M. |
| PO 8945 | Bell, W. C. | Pte., R.M. |
| CH 9576 | Barr, J. | Pte., R.M. |
| CH 9625 | Bland, A. | Pte., R.M. |
| | | |
| PLY 8685 | Carey, A. W. T. | Pte., R.M. |
| PLy 8643 | Clarke, W. | Pte., R.M. |
| CH 6170 | Cowell, J. | Pte., R.M. |
| CH 7847 | Churchill, C. | Corp., R.M. |
| PLY 8645 | Cowing, P. | Pte., R.M. (D) |
| | | |
| PLY 5358 | Dustan, J. W. | Captain, R.M.L.I. |
| PLY 2782 | Dawes, H. | Pte., R.M. |
| CH 8926 | Dodd, J. H. | Lance Sgt., R.M. |
| PO 8697 | Dunkley, F. | Pte., R.M. |
| PO 8866 | Dunnett, J. W. | Pte., R.M. |
| CH 8832 | Dean, W. B. | Pte., R.M. |
| PLY 7291 | Darke, W. C. | Pte., R.M. |
| PO 8928 | Eades, W. G. | Pte., R.M. |
| PO 4505 | Farmborough, J. | Pte., R.M. |
| CH 6887 | Fletcher, A. | Pte., R.M. |
| PLY 8598 | Good, R. | Pte., R.M. (P) |
| | Gray, A. H. | |
| | | |
| | Harris, W. A. | Captain, R.M.L.I. |
| | Harmer, C. D. O. | Lieut., R.M.L.I. (P) |
| PLY 8666 | Harries, C. | Pte., R.M. |
| PO 8933 | Hooten, H. | Pte., R.M. |
| PO 2379 | Handford, W. | Sgt., R.M. |
| CH 2330 | Hart, M. P. | Act. Sgt. Mjr., R.M. |
| CH 9679 | Hammond, H. S. J. | Pte., R.M. |

44

| | | |
|---|---|---|
| CH 9391 | Ireland, W. L. | Pte., R.M. |
| CH 9636 | Inch, F. A. | Pte., R.M. |
| CH 9578 | Johns, W. | Pte., R.M. |
| PO 8961 | Lord, W. | Pte., R.M. |
| PO 8923 | Lawson, A. | Pte., R.M. |
| | Maclurcan, J. L. R. | Major, R.M.L.I. |
| | Mayhew, C. L. | Lieut., R.M.L.I. |
| PO 8954 | Moloney, M. | Pte., R.M. |
| PLY 8674 | Moore, H. | Pte., R.M. |
| PO 8873 | McLoughlin, J. F. | Pte., R.M. (D) |
| CH 7592 | McLeod, H. E. | Pte., R.M. (D) |
| PLY 8618 | McKay, D. | Pte., R.M. |
| CH 7612 | Neller, F. J. | Pte., R.M. |
| CH 8712 | Padgett, L. | Corp., R.M. (D) |
| CH 9943 | Polkinghorne, E. F. | Bugler |
| CH 2155 | Philbrick, A. | Lance Corp. |
| PO 8931 | Phillimore, S. | Pte., R.M. |
| PLY 8277 | Rushman, A. | Pte., R.M. |
| PO 7061 | Reeve, A. M. | Corp., R.M. |
| PO 7792 | Rudgeley, F. | Pte., R.M. |
| CH 9629 | Randall, T. L. | Pte., R.M. |
| CH 3421 | Rogers, J. | Pte., R.M. |
| | Sparrow, H. S. R. | Staff Surgeon (P) |
| PLY 1872 | Sibley, J. | Pte., R.M. |
| CH 8796 | Smith, C. J. | Pte., R.M. |
| CH 9381 | Spooner, W. | Pte., R.M. |
| CH 8875 | Snook, C. | Pte., R.M. |
| CH 8751 | Stansfield, T. | Pte., R.M. |
| PO 7148 | Tidmas, G. | Pte., R.M. |
| CH 4604 | Timms, G. | Pte., R.M. |
| PO 8858 | Tulk, A. | Corp., R.M. |
| CH 7225 | Thompson, W. G. | Pte., R.M. |
| PLY 3421 | Thatcher, E. C. | Sgt., R.M. |
| CH 5673 | Tassell, C. | Pte., R.M. |
| PLY 8657 | Wood, F. G. | Pte., R.M. |

(D) = Duplicate issued.
(P) = Presented by H.M. the King 8.3.1902

45

Chinese Christians flee from the wrath of the Boxers as war looms ahead. British sailors can be seen helping them onto the boats

# THE TAKU FORTS

The Pei-ho snakes its way, with two giant loops, to Tong-ku, where is situated the railway station for Tientsin. Tong-ku is a distance of about three miles as the crow flies, and five by river from the coast and Gulf of Pe-chi-li. The Taku Forts, which guarded the entrance, were forbidding to any assailant. From seaward it was almost impossible to attack the forts because of the miles of mud-banks which, uncovered at half tide, stretched before the 'South' and the 'New' Forts which lined a mile and a half of the south bank coastline. The North Fort commanded the entrance on the opposite bank 200 yards across. Its eastern face lay half a mile behind the sand and seashells that then merged with mud banks and the sea. Batteries extended for a further mile inland along the river from the North Fort. Less than a mile from the final Reach of the Pei-ho to Tong-ku and set inland to the west, were three small forts (inexplicably unmanned). In the second loop of the river was the Imperial Dockyard berthing four Chinese destroyers.

The little squadron of Allied ships which were to engage the forts had, however, passed the mouth of the Pei-ho and were moored at Tong-ku and under the guns of the main North Battery. Effectively, much of the battle was to be fought across the land encompassed by the river loop to the North Batteries and Fort, and against the rear of the South Forts.

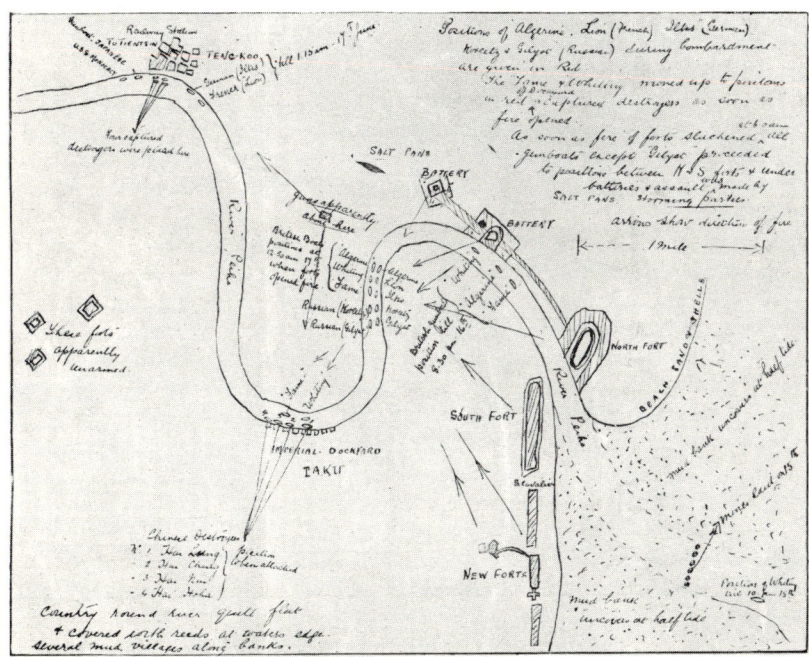

Plan of the bombardment of the Taku Forts
(Facsimile of sketch by an eye-witness on board a British warship)

47

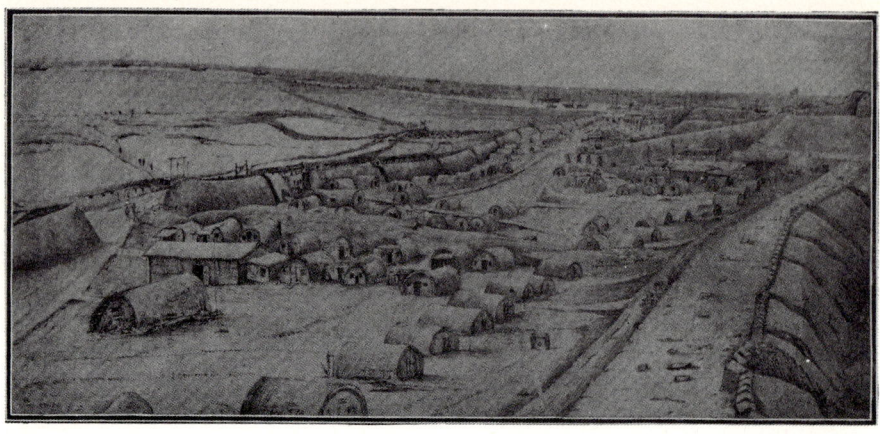

### The South Fort at Taku

The Europeans had had previous experience of the Taku Forts. In 1857 the Second China War had broken out and by 1858 it looked as if the War was over: Canton was captured in January of 1858, Yeh was caught and sent into exile to Calcutta, and Lord Elgin demanded that the Treaty of Peace should be signed at Peking. The envoys chosen to perform this function in the Celestial City arrived off the Pei-ho with their full ceremonial uniforms ready for a pomp and splendour ritual. But they found no satin-dressed mandarins waiting to welcome them. Instead they got a broadside from the Taku Forts.

After Admiral Sir Michael Seymour had forced an entrance on May 20 the Chinese surrendered, a bar 'Taku Forts 1858' being later added to the China Medal. (Vice-Admiral Sir Edward H. Seymour, Commander-in-Chief of the China Station in 1900, was a cousin of Admiral Michael Seymour and had taken part in the Second China War. As a midshipman he was on *Calcutta*'s launch when it sank in action at Fatshan; and he qualified for the bar 'Taku Forts 1858').

Under the terms of the subsequent Treaty, Britain and France were to have ambassadors at Peking. Sir Frederick Bruce, intent on taking up his assignment entered the Pei-ho a year later only to be fired upon from the Taku Forts. On June 18 and 19 of that year Admiral Sir James Hope fought his ships against the Forts. He failed, suffered heavy casualties and had to withdraw. Despite the great courage shown there was no bar to the China medal on that occasion. It has been said that Queen Victoria had acidly remarked on a similar occasion that she did not award bars for defeats!

By 1860 the British and French forces had gathered sufficient strength for another all-out onslaught. On August 21 the Taku Forts were captured for the second time and the bar 'Taku Forts 1860' was added to the medal; making it possible for a recipient of the Second China War Medal to have both 'Taku Forts' bars.

This last action was forty years previous to the Third China War. The Taku defences were, at that time, described in a private letter from General Sir George Colley who had taken part in the battle.

'All these forts present a most extraordinary contrast of strength and weakness, science and folly. Alongside of enormous guns, eight- and ten-inch, beautifully cast in gunmetal, and not worth less than £1,000 each, are to be seen bows, crossbows, and catapults that might have been used at the siege of Troy. In the same way, with a most defective plan, the forts have been so strengthened and are so massive as to be almost impregnable from the sea. The large southern fort alone mounts 210 guns; of these some, it is true, are things made of bars of iron bound together with hoops, such as Edward III may have used; but certainly a hundred are guns of the heaviest calibre used; 32, 68 and 80-pounders. One gun, which is valued at £2,000 is a perfect specimen of Chinese labour without science. It is of pure copper, beautifully cast, but the metal made of exactly the same thickness all the way from the breech to the muzzle; and even the breech twice as thick as is necessary; the consequence is, about five tons of metal have been used to turn out a gun which will throw a shot about the same weight to a shorter distance than one of our 24-pounders requiring about one ton of metal.'

In 1900 the Forts had been much improved and were certainly better armed. The Southern Forts mounted about 120 guns, most of which were of modern pattern and were long range. The great network of defences covered around three miles and was designed for the protection of Tientsin, the seaport of the capital, Peking. The earthenworks were exceptionally strong, probably because the inhabitants of North China lived mainly in mud-built houses and were expert in the use of that material.

The fortifications contained cement and concrete galleries with iron framings to the casemates. The North Fort was well casemated and mounted about 50 guns, while the main North Battery had some 30 guns. The New Forts on the south bank contained many of the latest and heaviest Krupp quick-firing guns. These included 4.7-inch Krupps and 5-inch Vavaseurs. German engineers had been employed to strengthen the defences – and now their military colleagues had to fight against their handiwork.

Maintenance and manning was not, it appears, controlled from a central authority in Peking, but left to the discretion of the local governor, whose pocket was involved. Consequently in times of peace he maintained a small staff comprised largely of his friends and relations. With characteristic Chinese apathy to eventualities, they did as little as was essential to maintain the Forts.

However, in the early part of June the Peking authorities took over and Imperial troops were drafted into the forts. It is believed that about 3,000 regular Chinese troops garrisoned the Forts on June 17. They included men from the province of Hu-nan, and came under the command of General Liu.

The Chinese armed forces were effectively in five classes: 1 – the Bannermen; 2 – the Green Standard Troops of the Territorial Army; 3 – the Braves, an off-shoot of Gordon's 'Ever Victorious Army'; 4 – the Chien-Chun, a type of Imperial Guard organised by Li Hung Chang and trained by German officers; 5 – local troops or levies.

The Chien-Chun were, of course, efficient, brave and well trained. The men of the Chien-Chun drafted to the Taku Forts were to win the begrudging admiration of the Allies for their courage and tenacity. Their handling of the guns left a lot to be desired; but then they had only a matter of days to become conversant with them. They probably accounted for most of the Allied casualties.

For some time previous, the complicity of the Dowager-Empress with the Boxers had been uncertain; but the downgrading of several high-ranking mandarins following defeat at the Taku Forts speaks for itself.

Even from the landward side there was little cover for the assailants. One writer described it: 'The country here is dreary in the extreme, and is nothing more than a mud flat. Not a single tree or rocky outcrop relieves the dull monotony of the surroundings. The only industries are fishing and the production of salt from brine pans. A mile or so higher up the

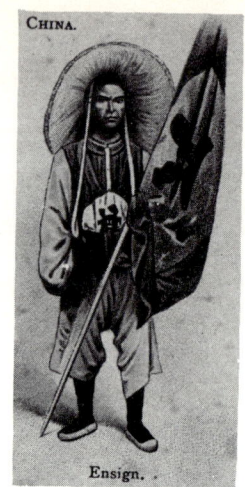

Chinese Imperial Guard

Chinese Ensign

river is the village of Tong-ku on which the railway lines from Peking and Shan-hai-kwan respectively converge.'

In the early part of June a powerful fleet formed by eight different nations, old friends and old foes, lay about 13 miles from the Taku Forts, effectively out of range.

The British large ships of the Fleet anchored off Taku on June 16 were HMS *Barfleur, Alacrity, Centurion, Endymion, Aurora* and *Orlando.*

What worried their commanders most was the problem of shore communications. They had internal problems with languages of eight different nations, but worse, they had heard next to nothing about events on the mainland.

It was known that Admiral Sir E. H. Seymour, whose flagship was HMS *Centurion*, was leading a 2,000 strong International Relief Force towards Peking to succour the Legations. It was supposed that this expedition was now in trouble as since June 13 no communication had been made from the commander-in-chief to his base at Tientsin.

During the night of the 14th the fleet learned that all railway carriages and rolling stock had been ordered to be sent up the line for the purpose of bringing down a Chinese army to Tong-ku. This indicated that Tientsin was also in trouble. If Taku was barred to the Allies it would be only a matter of time before the mainland forces ran out of ammunition and supplies. Then the Legations, Seymour's expedition and the settlement at Tientsin would be mercilessly wiped out. It was a serious situation and a council of admirals was summoned by Vice-Admiral Hiltebrandt, Commander-in-Chief of the Russian Squadron. Rear Admiral James Bruce, commanding HMS *Barfleur*, attended from Britain, and admirals represented Germany, France and the United States, while senior officers attended on behalf of Italy, Austria and Japan.

The big ships of the fleet were virtually impotent because of the Taku Bar. This treacherous stretch could be as shallow as three feet at low tide and only reached a maximum of about eleven feet at high tide. Consequently small ships were able to cross the bar and come within range of the Taku Forts which guarded the entrance to the Pei-ho. There were ten Allied ships in the river or just outside at this time being the only fighting ships able to cross the bar.

Instructions were sent to them, with immediate effect, to prevent any railway plant being taken away from Tong-ku, or the Chinese army from reaching that place, which would, of course, cut off communication lines with Tientsin. In the event that the Chinese attempted either of those courses the little ships were to use force and to destroy the Taku Forts.

This was easier said than done.

HMS *Algerine* had six 4-inch guns: HMS *Fame* and *Whiting*, (destroyer-torpedo boats) would be occupied capturing the Chinese destroyers: the *Iltis* had eight 3.4-inch quick-firing guns. The Fench *Lion* had two 5.5-inch guns and the largest gun was a 9-inch on the bows of *Bobr*, the Russian 'flagship' of the little fleet. *Koreetch* and *Gilyak* were the other Russian gunboats, armed with two 8-inch and one 6-inch on the former, and one 4-inch, two 2.6-inch and four 1.8-inch in the latter.

*Atago* (Japan) and *Monocacy* (USA) did not take part in the gun battle so the array of Allied guns against those of the Forts was not very impressive.

The Chinese did not, in the event, take any action which would oblige the small ships to take offensive action. But the news did not get any better. Information began coming through in the evening and during the night of the 15th that the mouth of the Pei-ho was being protected against the Allies by electric mines.

Several reputable writers on the Boxer Rebellion have always qualified this (Peter Fleming states 'allegedly') but there seems no doubt that these mines were used. An entry in the Royal Navy List 1914 (145) January for COURTIS, E. G. states: 'Joined Royal Navy 7th December 1888; warrant officer, 1st November 1898; served in 'Algerine' during Boxer Rebellion in China, 1900: during the bombardment of the Taku Forts was Gunnery Officer of the ship, and succeeded in remounting a 3 Pr. Q.F. gun, under fire, in 15 minutes; later, having observed a line of electric observation mines ahead, Mr. Courtis went away in a dinghy with one man, and personally performed the dangerous service of destroying five of the enemy's mines by cutting wires, removing detonators and primers, and drowning the mines, thus probably saving many lives . . .'

The prospect of mines interfering with operations was, in any event, sufficient for the senior officers to hold another council of war. The same naval officers met on board the *Rossia* in the forenoon of June 16 and it was concluded that the situation had now reached a point of extreme gravity which called for action. Information came through which put the matter beyond doubt. The Forts were being provisioned and reinforced.

There was, however, one dissenting voice, Admiral Kempff of the United States. Burt Firschfeld, in *Fifty-five Days of Terror*, tells us that the Admiral addressed the council: 'Gentlemen, I am obliged to point out that no declaration of war has been made against China by any of the powers. The attack you plan would automatically constitute such a declaration. I, therefore, stand opposed to the suggested action. The forces under my command will not participate'.

What Admiral Kempff did not know at that time, of course, was that while he was speaking American marines were fighting for their lives in Admiral Seymour's expeditionary force; and looked very much like losing them.

The *Monocacy*, a turtle-shaped wooden paddle-steamer of 1863, with insignificant firepower, did not take part in the battle at all, even though it was struck by shell-fire from the Forts. Peter Fleming in *The Siege at Peking* accounts for this failure to participate: 'The instructions given by Washington to Admiral Kempff did not include authority to take part in hostilities against China, and it is possible that he had wind of a signal sent a few days earlier to the Navy Department from the Philippines by Admiral Remey, the Senior Commander of

The United States Ship *Monocacy*

the Asiatic Station; this accused Kempff of "co-operating foreign powers to an extent incompatible interests American Government". Kempff was criticised afterwards; "at first" one of his officers said, "there was considerable feeling against him for standing out of an elegant fight when one was on hand". But he was an enterprising officer whose hands were tied by his Government's policy, and he probably sympathised with the paddle-steamer's captain, Commander Wise, who wrote to him: "I feel a natural regret, shared no doubt by the officers, that duty and orders prevented the old Monocacy from giving her ancient smooth-bores a last chance".'

Admiral Kempff's view was not shared by the rest of the council. An ultimatum was sent to the Viceroy of Chili at Tientsin and also to the Commandant of the Forts, saying that in consequence of the danger to the Allies on the mainland, by the actions of the Chinese Authorities, the Allies proposed to temporarily occupy the Taku Forts, 'by consent or by force'. The ultimatum expired at 2.00 am on June 17.

The necessary orders were transmitted to the commanding officers of the little ships who thus found themselves in a truly David and Goliath position. The Allied squadron of men-of-war inside the bar immediately held their own conference on board *Bobr* under the senior naval officer, the Russian Post Captain of *Bobr*, Captain Dobrovolsky. At that meeting battle plans were laid and it was agreed to take up fighting positions by 4.00 am and open fire on the Forts at that hour should they not have surrendered before then.

HMS *Algerine* took up its station at once, shifting berth at 8.00 pm and prepared for action.

With the events of the Sino-Japanese War fresh in their minds it is doubtful whether the Allies really expected the Chinese to take the initiative. On paper the Chinese looked superior, but in practice the Allies had some reason to rely upon the very high standard of efficiency of its own fighting forces compared to the poorly trained and led Chinese troops. Nevertheless, the Allies were taking no more chances than were absolutely necessary.

The forthcoming battle had three phases.

1. Six Allied ships would wage a running gun battle with the forts using the river as best they could to prevent accurate gun-laying by the Fort batteries, and with the objective of silencing the fire-power of the forts.
2. Land forces would storm the forts and occupy them.
3. HMS *Fame* and HMS *Whiting* would capture the four modern Chinese destroyers berthed in the Chinese Naval Dockyard. They presented a threat to the whole operation if committed to battle.

The men of HMS *Centurion* landing for action

On the eve of battle the fleet outside the Taku Bar had a busy time, as is evidenced by the logs of the British ships. It is also apparent that they did not overlook the possibility of the Imperial Chinese destroyers being handled properly, and making a torpedo attack on the fleet. HMS *Orlando*'s log for June 16 shows that the foreign population were beginning to get distinctly nervous: 'Received on board four missionaries and one infant with servants'. Then, at 1500 hours: 'Landed 103 officers and men for Active Service including Lieut. Hyde, Messrs. Phillips and Higgins, W.O.s and Mids.' HMS *Barfleur*, which would be in the line of attack should the Chinese torpedoes come, recorded the arrival on June 16 of more big ships: '0445. Russian 'Admiral Kornilof' man-of-war arrived. 10.30 German Kaiserin Augusta arrived.' In the afternoon: 'Landed for storming party for Taku Forts Lieut. Williams, four Midshipmen, 54 seamen and 26 marines.' At 1.00 pm the brief entry: 'Manned and armed ship – watch standing by their guns'.

HMS *Endymion* also had a busy day. 'Pm. Employed equipping and telling off landing party to assist in attacking Taku Forts. 1500. Sent landing party of 31 men and Mid. Briggs under the command of Lieut. A. R. Hulbert to Flagship. 1530. Landing party went in to Taku in a tug'. Men from *Endymion* had also worked throughout the night for a log entry for June 15 at 2335 shows: 'Sent to Barfleur the following ammunition: .303 rifle 15,000 rounds; 45 D.A. fuzes; 150 9 pdr charges, 150 friction tubes, 43 common shell, 66 case shot'. The fleet was seeing to it that its landing parties were well armed.

HMS *Centurion* was the flagship of Admiral Seymour who was leading the relief expedition and had taken nearly all the available hands for his Naval Brigade. But the ship did not intend to be left out of the battle altogether and the ship's log has an entry: '14.30 Sent 7 marines and 6 seamen fully equipped, 3 cases of gun cotton to tug for landing'. At 2115: 'Watch manned and armed ship. Placed extra lookouts'. HMS *Aurora*'s men were also busy at around midnight on June 15 sending to *Barfleur* for landing, ammunition for rifles and 9-pounder field gun. Early on June 16 the *Alacrity* had shifted to berth above *Barfleur* which was being used as a staging ship for landing fighting supplies. HMS *Aurora*'s log for June 16 has a pm entry: 'Sent to *Barfleur* equipped for landing 48 men with 2 mids. under command of Lieut. T. W. Kemp with three days stores, provisions and ammunition. Stationed hands remaining on board at Quick Firing and machine guns. Got up ready supply ammunition and prepared for resisting torpedo boat attack.'

Commander of *Alacrity*, Christopher Cradock, was appointed to take charge of the Allied forces on shore at the attack on Taku Forts. With the British landing parties he waited patiently in HMS *Algerine* for the deadline to approach.

All was ready. The Allies did not expect anything to happen until 4.00 am on June 17, the time they had set, two hours after the expiry of the ultimatum, to take the Taku Forts. Lolling gently at its mooring HMS *Algerine* was so near to the forts that Chinese gunners could be seen grinning down at them. G. A. Henty, famous author of children's books was a war correspondent in the Boxer Rebellion. He said: 'We thought that, as usual, messages would be exchanged, and that the thing would drag on a little before anything serious came of it. The "Algerine" had her ventilators up, masts all standing, and yards crossed. The Germans on the Iltis had landed their boats and ventilators some days before; the Lion had housed her ventilators but still had her yards crossed'. There seemed to be a general feeling that the Chinese would not dare to take them on! It may well have been that the Allied commanders anticipated the Chinese would concede at the last minute. At 9.00 pm five hours before the deadline, a long searchlight armoured train puffed its way laboriously across the plains. It was scouting to see if any Chinese military movements were being made. It was commanded by Lieutenants Kirkpatrick and Riley and was armed with a 12-pounder. Hotchkiss, two Maxims and a hundred men drawn from the German, British and French contingents. A German engineer from the *Iltis* was the engine driver, and British sailors did the stoking. The Chinese crew had disappeared.

As the searchlight stabbed into the murky night it was clearly visible over the flat plains and for nearly three hours both Chinese and Allies must have watched it with hypnotic fascination till it finally disappeared from view in the direction of Tientsin.

Almost as if that was the signal, the Chinese opened fire. It was 12.50 am, well over an hour before the expiration of the ultimatum. Some contemporary reporters referred to the Chinese as 'treacherous' for such an act. But whereas in medieval days times for battle were often set by mutual consent, it was hardly an attitude which could be expected at the opening of the twentieth century. World War II tacticians would have approved.

The Allies got over their surprise very quickly. The port watch of HMS *Algerine* had just turned in. Hardly were they in their hammocks than they were running to general quarters in whatever state of dress they could manage. The Commander of HMS *Algerine* recorded in his official letter on the battle: 'At 12.50 am all the forts opened fire and we engaged the enemy'. G. A. Henty said: 'No return shot came from her and it was evident that she was taken as much by surprise as we were. It was about five minutes before the Algerine replied'. This is supported by the ship's log: '0050 Forts opened fire simultaneously on Allied Squadron. Went to Quarters. 055: Returned the fire of the forts.'

As the staccato of gun flashes bit into the sky HMS *Fame* and *Whiting* slipped silently from their moorings and moved upstream to their targets, the Chinese destroyers. The success of their part of the action was crucial. The German *Iltis* and the French *Lion* were just below Tong-ku and the *Monocacy* and *Atago* near them. The Chinese imperial destroyers lay between those four ships and the rest of the sqadron and were well able to prevent them from joining up.

In what must have been an adventurous expedition, Lieut Roger Keyes commanding *Fame*, and Lieut Mackenzie, commanding *Whiting*, had scouted the Chinese dockyard the previous evening to examine the lay of the land. They found the destroyers moored head and stern in single line off the south steep-to bank with wire hawsers laid out from each bow and quarter.

Roger Keyes, who years later was to become Admiral of the Fleet, judged the distance between the fourth and second destroyers to be about one and a half cables so he planned for *Fame* to weigh at 2.00 am followed by *Whiting* at one and a half cables distance. Both would tow whalers, each containing boarding parties of 12 men under Lieut Wilfred Tomkinson (*Fame*) and Lieut John Alfred Moreton (*Whiting*). The plan was to pass well out in the stream so that the Chinese would think the British ships were proceeding up river to Tong-ku. When HMS *Fame*'s bow was abreast of No.4 destroyer, HMS *Whiting* would be abreast of No.2 and the warships would sheer in hard to port and board the Chinese vessels over their bows, each whaler boarding the next astern. The main armaments which would have appeared to be innocently facing ahead upstream would now be able to cover the boarding parties, and riflemen would also give covering fire.

The plan had to be put into action immediately when the Chinese opened the battle. Instead of steaming serenely upstream the little fighting ships ploughed up the bow waves at speed with enemy shot falling all about them. Other than that, the plan worked well.

In his operational despatch to his commanding officer (Commander R. H. Johnston Stewart, HMS *Algerine*) written immediately after the battle, Keyes wrote: 'After a slight

The French gunboat *Lion*

resistance and the exchange of a few shots, the crews were driven overboard or below hatches; there were a few killed and wounded; our casualties, nil. No damage was done to the prizes, the 'Fame's' bow was slightly bent when we closed to board, and the "Whiting" was struck by a projectile about 4 to 5 inches abreast a coal bunker. This was evidently fired from a mud battery on the bend between Taku and Tong-ku, which fired in all about 30 shots at us, none of the others striking, though several coming very close. I could not reply for fear of striking the Russian gun vessels lying behind it. There was a good deal of sniping from the dockyard, so I directed all cables of prizes to be slipped and proceeded to tow them up to Tong-ku. At this point, Mr. Macrae, the manager of the "Tug and Lighter Company" came to my assistance; I cannot speak too highly of this gentleman's assistance, he took one destroyer off my hands, as did another of the same company's tugs for the "Whiting". In the former case Mr. Macrae had to use force, with the assistance of one of my men, on the Chinese crew, most of whom tried to jump overboard when we came under fire of the mud-battery. In the latter case, Mr. Mayne, Midshipman of the Barfleur, was in command of a guard of seamen with a maxim, and also did very well.'

It must have been one of the last occasions that British blue-jackets were armed with cutlasses when boarding a 'prize' ship. They found the torpedoes were in the tubes, but warheads had not been fitted. Ammunition for quick-firing guns in two of the destroyers was on deck ready for use. It would seem that the British had got there just in time, and that in another few minutes the Chinese ships would have been at general quarters – and presented a much more difficult task.

By 5.00 am the Chinese destroyers, now prizes of the Royal Navy, were securely berthed at Tong-ku. But Roger Keyes still had another job to do. Midshipman Mayne had been put in charge of a tug with despatches and stores for Tientsin, but his Chinese crew would not pass a fort 12 miles up the river at LunChang. So *Fame* and *Whiting* proceeded, intending to force a passage. They found no opposition and were able to return to Taku.

Right: Lieut C. Mackenzie (HMS *Whiting*), Left: Lieut J.A. Moreton (HMS *Whiting*) pictured moments after they had led their cutlass-brandishing seamen over the sides of two Chinese destroyers and captured them during the Battle of the Taku Forts.

Lieut C. Mackenzie, in his report of the action, wrote: 'I boarded and captured the two (Chinese destroyers) lying downstream at about 1.30 am and as soon as prize crews were got on board and the four wire hawsers, with which each was secured, either cut, or the anchor attached to it weighed, I towed one to Tong-ku out of reach of the shell-fire of the Forts, and was just returning to tow the other up (she had great difficulty in weighing her anchor) when she came in sight, in tow of the tug *Fa Wan*.

In towing one of the prizes to Tong-ku, a mud fort, hitherto silent, opened a hot fire on us, and the "Whiting" received one 5-inch shot in the hull just forward of the engine-room bulkhead, starboard side, passing through bunker (full) carrying away wing-door of boiler and damaging several tubes and putting No. 4 boiler out of action, otherwise not causing any more damage.'

HMS *Whiting* had been very fortunate. The Chinese gunners, in their excitement, had forgotten the formality of fusing the shell and it did not explode. It was recovered, given a place of honour on deck, and photographed many times. Had it exploded the damage could have been much more severe. *Whiting* was sent to Nagasaki for repairs and returned to Pei-ho on July 9.

The captured Chinese destroyers (German-built) were the *Hai Lung*, *Hai Ching*, *Hai-Nin* and *Hai-Hoha*. One was taken into service by the Royal Navy. The others were given to Russia, Germany and France. A somewhat ungrateful Admiralty refused to grant prize-money on the grounds that no state of war existed between China and Great Britain.

Lieut Moreton of HMS *Whiting*, who had led a boarding party in one of the whalers, took the first destroyer 'in a very able manner, and succeeded in raising steam and going to quarters for action in about two hours from the time of boarding'.

The *Iltis* and *Lion* swept downstream to join battle with the Forts the moment the Chinese

The shell which damaged the *Whiting*

destroyers were no longer a threat to their passage. The *Monocacy* and the *Atago* stayed at Tong-ku. The *Atago* was an old iron gunboat with obsolete armament and contented itself with assisting land operations at Tong-ku.

This meant that only six ships engaged the Forts: HMS *Algerine*, an old sloop, the *Iltis* a German ship very similar to *Algerine*; the *Gilyak* a modern Russian gunboat; *Bobr* and *Koreetz*, two Russian old steel gunboats, and the *Lion* a French gunboat which had the distinction of being the oldest gunboat in the squadron.

HMS *Algerine* had been the first to return fire. It was to be a long drawn out battle unlike the quick, decisive, part of *Fame* and *Whiting*. The ship's log of HMS *Algerine* has an entry on that day which gives an idea of the duration: 'Expended during bombardment: 4" QF Cordite 576 cartridges; Shell A.P. filled, 92; Common pointed 470; shrapnel 12, Lyddite 2. Three pounder Q.F. Cordite 390 cartridges, Powder, 32 cartridges; .45 machine gun 1,336 cartridges; .303 6,800; pistol Webley, 2,814'. Well over 1,500 shells had been fired at the Forts from this one ship. In addition the fighting tops were manned by machine-gunners and riflemen. The fact that 2,814 pistol shots were fired indicates the close range at which much of the action took place.

The Forts from the north

A correspondent of *The Times* was to write: '... It was useless to cheer now in the continuous din of battle. Here and there in the smoke and spray a glimpse would be had of a gallant little gunboat – the *Algerine*, her decks alive with men stripped to the waist and working desperately; upon the bridge over the quarter deck a little group of Englishmen stood as calmly as if they were steaming up the Solent ...'

The British landing party which had been sent in by tug from the outer anchorages on June 16, had been supplied each with 100 rounds of ammunition and three days' provisions, and had joined HMS *Algerine* for the purpose of being berthed prior to being landed for action. They were to land abreast of HMS *Algerine* and meet the other forces marching from Tongku at a rendezvous on the military road. The moment the action started the commander of *Algerine* ordered the landing party into the boats in order that his decks could be cleared for action.

But the Chinese were not permitted to interfere with planned priorities merely because they had started the battle earlier than expected. 'Each man of the force received a ration of optional cocoa, handed down into the boats before shoving off, and this was consumed before the boats were allowed to leave.' (Cradock).

R. H. Johnstone Stewart, commanding *Algerine* wrote of the action: 'I directed my fire with 4-inch guns on the North West Fort, but finding that much ammunition was being expended, and that the shooting in the moonlight was not very accurate, I simply kept one 4-inch firing. I did not use my searchlight as I judged that it would only draw the fire of the south fort on the ship ... At about 2.45 am I received a message from Commander Cradock that the landing party were about to assault the North West Fort, and requesting the ships not to fire on it, which message was passed on to the other allied ships by boat, and the fire continued on the South and North Forts. At about 3.45 am another message was received from Commander Cradock to the effect that the North West Fort was practically untouched

The German *Iltis* from a German cigarette card set produced shortly after the battle. Awarded the Pour le Merite for the action – the artist managed to have it on the bows during the action!

and too strong for them to assault. It was now daylight, and I opened fire on the fort with all my starboard 4-inch guns, together with the Iltis whose firing was very well directed. By about 4.30 am the return fire had practically ceased, and shortly afterwards the fort was carried by assault.

At about 5 o'clock I hoisted the pre-arranged signal, and when it had been repeated by the foreign ships, I weighed at about 5.30 am and, closely followed by the Iltis and the other ships, except Gilyak, which had a compartment full of water and could not move, I led the squadron down the river, firing on the North Fort with my forecastle guns, and engaging the South Forts with the remainder of my starboard broadside. The North Fort made no return, and had been deserted by the garrison, but the fire from the South Fort was very heavy, and it was only by God's mercy that we were not hulled. It was at this period that all casualties occurred.'

At 7.10 am HMS *Algerine* ceased fire. It had been a long battle. The German *Iltis* had made haste to join the battle and was in the thick of it. Built at Schichau in Danzig in 1897 it was modern, had a crew of 125 and was 900 tons. The ship was awarded the Pour la Merit – which decoration, in giant size, was placed on the bows.

The *Times* correspondent watched as '. . . without hardly a word being spoken the *Iltis* cast off from the wharf and, quickly gathering way, steamed rapidly down the stream. Without a single light or sign of life about her, in absolute silence she sped swiftly towards the foe. As she rounded the bend and opened up the Taku Reach, and the vessels below saw the gallant German coming to their aid, cheer after cheer rose first from the *Gilyak*, then the *Koreetch* and *Bobr*, and there was no mistaking the ringing welcome that went up from the *Algerine*.'

The *Iltis* and *Lion* formed line with the other gunboats and the six of them, at an average range of certainly not more than a mile, engaged the whole of the Forts now firing heavily from their western faces.

*Bobr* was perhaps the luckiest of the Allied fleet suffering hardly any casualties yet taking equal chances and running equal risks, keeping up a galling fire from her big 9-inch bow gun.

The *Gilyak* suffered the most, principally because her commanding officer was unable to resist the temptation to 'play with his new toy'. He had a newly installed and most up-to-date searchlight. While it helped the other ships to aim it drew a heavy fire on his ship. From the

The Russian gunboat *Gilyak*

shelter of the mud huts in the Taku village, Chinese riflemen sniped at her decks causing casualties. The searchlight was soon extinguished as shown by the ship's log of HMS *Barfleur*: '0100. Observed searchlight on River. 0108 searchlight extinguished.'

The Allied ships began to get hit. The *Gilyak* was struck by a heavy shell on her starboard beam at the water-line, listed heavily to starboard as water began pouring in, and unable to move, though still plying her guns, ceased to be a real factor in the bombardment. The *Iltis* moving down to the South Forts was struck by a shell on her starboard bow which, passing inboard, cut into the forward boiler. The ship was at once engulfed in a mass of steam, her captain put out of action, and she had to be beached on the Taku side of the Fort Reach. *Gilyak* was hit again by a shell which exploded charges in one of her smaller magazines causing death and destruction.

The *Lion* made a spectacular sight with its four giant tricolours flying at the mastheads as it steamed this way and that to assist *Bobr* and *Koreetch* as they maintained a continuous cannonade.

Viceroy Yu Lu, whose friendship with the British was such that he was offered asylum on board a British warship 'in the event of his being in personal danger owing to his loyalty to the British' had the unenviable task of reporting on these events to the Empress Dowager. He reported what the Empress wanted to hear. Two foreign warships had been put out of action; but he omitted to mention that the Forts had nevertheless been taken by the foreign powers. So on June 21, when his despatch was received, the Imperial Court were blissfully unaware of the true position.

The Chinese, on balance, appeared to be holding their own. Two of the better ships on the small Allied squadron were temporarily, at least, out of action. But the Fort gunners were to suffer two extreme mishaps. At around 4.30 am an explosion occurred in one of the Southern Forts. It caused a big fire and un-nerved many of the garrison. The Chinese recovered well from this explosion which only checked their fire for a short time. Soon after 5 am some of the heavy casemated guns on the north bastion of the South Fort were slued so far round that their blast could be sent up the Reach. By this time too, the Chinese had become aware that in the excitement and bustle many of their shells were being fired unfused, and thus failing to explode. Now a much greater proportion of their shells were exploding.

HMS *Algerine*'s commander had good reason to refer to 'God's mercy' for just as the Chinese shells began to take their toll the second explosion occurred, at 0600 in the main magazine of the South Fort. This explosion was so devastating, its vibrations reaching the ships at the Taku Bar, that both sides stopped fighting instantly. Chinese and Allies gazed in awe as smoke and debris billowed a thousand feet into the sky. Many of the men ashore were blinded by the dust and smoke. The Allies were the first to recover from the shock and with a rousing cheer rejoined battle. The Chinese, many of whom were superstitious, must have felt that their Gods were against them, and joined battle with less enthusiasm, and less fire-power.

Keen eyes on the warships at the Taku Bar logged events: HMS *Barfleur*: '0430. Observed a large fire in Taku. 0605 a very heavy explosion occurred in the vicinity of the South Fort'. HMS *Aurora*: '0415. Explosion occurred with vivid flame at Taku. 0555 Second large explosion with dense cloud of dust and smoke at Taku'.

It was history repeating itself. In 1860 the Manchu general Sankolinson wrote that the loss of the Taku Forts was due to 'the unfortunate explosion of a powder magazine'.

But even without these explosions the tenacious Allied squadron had certainly battered the Forts to a point where the fire-power was drastically lessened. It now remained for the landing parties to storm the Forts with fixed bayonets.

Commander Cradock had landed his men in half an hour under heavy shellfire but had completed the operation by 2.30 am without mishap.

The Allied assault force consisted of: British: 23 officers, 298 men (commanding officer, Commander Christopher Cradock HMS *Alacrity*) Total 321; German: 3 officers, 130 men (commanding officer, Commander Pohl, HIMS *Hansa*) Total 133; Japanese: 4 officers, 240 men (commanding officer, Commander Hattori IJS *Kasagi*) Total 244; Russian: 2 officers 157 men (commanding officer, Lieutenant Stankewitch, 12th Regiment Tirailleurs d'Orient, *Luberie*) Total 159; Italian: 1 officer, 24 men (commanding officer, Lieutenant J. Tanca, IMS *Calabria*) Total 25; Austrian: 2 officers, 20 men (commanding officer, Lieutenant Ernst Stenner *Zenta*) (*The Gazette* of October 5, 1900 incorrectly gives Lieut Ernst Tatniums Quenta) Total 23. A grand total of 904 officers and men.

In his report to Rear-Admiral J. Bruce, Cradock wrote: 'It was arranged that, after an effective bombardment, the N.W. Fort should be the first to be attacked, then the N. Fort (on the same side of the river), and finally, the long string of south forts on the other bank; before the advance, it was agreed that half the British should lead the firing line with the Italians on the left, Germans, Japanese, and that the other half of the British, the Russians and Austrians, should form the supports, and reserves.

The German and Japanese commanders were pleased to propose that I should direct proceedings, which I had the great honour to do.

At 2.45 am when some 250 yards from the north face of the Fort, the advance commenced, deploying from the right, which flank rested on the river bank; the whole ground a thousand yards this side of the fort was hard mud, but unfortunately quite flat, without a vestige of cover.

The objective of the British was to force or scale the west gate, and this done, to endeavour to gain an entrance into the inner fort, by means of another gate, the whereabouts of which was not quite clear. To do this they were to advance in skirmishing order, to within 50 yards of the moat on the north face, then close on the right, and swinging round the corner of the fort along the military road, the right flank leading in loose formation, seeking what cover the right bank might afford, and charge on the west entrance.

The advance continued until within 1,000 yards of the fort, when I could plainly see that, owing to the darkness, it had suffered little from gun fire, and was practically intact, no guns being silenced. I therefore halted the men and returned myself to consult the other commanding officers as to continuing; it was at once unanimously agreed, that to take it in its present condition, all its guns being still in action, would entail a serious and unnecessary loss of life, and it was therefore decided to retire slightly for the cover afforded by the bend in the river, and wait until the fort was further reduced.

It was not until 4.30 am half an hour after dawn, that the heavy ordnance was finally silenced by the ships, although two field guns which had been previously silenced, now commenced to play on the attacking party.

The second formation of attack was different to the first; on the previous retirement the Alacrity and Endymion's men had been ordered to remain 300 yards to the front, as an observation party. They were under cover of a small rising, and shortly before the advance were joined by the Russians on the left.

In the firing line were the Alacrity's and Endymion's on the right, Russians on the left, and Italians in loose formation immediately on the right flank, the military road slightly interfering with their getting into line. The Barfleur's closed in the rear of the fighting line, reinforcing while the charge was sounded. The foreign forces and the remainder of the British were in close support, the Russians inclining to the left to make their attack on the right rear.

When the charge was sounded the Japanese doubled up from the supports in column of route along the road, and raced with the British along the intervening 300 yards to the west gate, the two nations scaling the parapet together[1].

Part of the British force also gained an entrance through two gun ports, and over a low part of the ramparts to the right of the gates which were held by my officers through the instrumentality of Lieutenant Duncan of HMS Algerine, who from previous observation on shore had found these weak spots. The inner and second gate was forced by rifle fire from the British and Japanese, and this done the fort was practically ours.'

Midshipman C.C. Dix, who years later as a Lieutenant was to write *The World's Navies in the Boxer Rebellion (China 1900)* wrote of the attack: 'Drill book tactics fell to the ground. The force started at a steady double, halted at 800 yards and fired two volleys; the same at 500 yards; once more at 300 yards; then "the charge" was sounded! The order "supports into the fighting line"; "fix bayonets"; and away we all dashed.

There was a race for the two flag-staffs; the Chinese yellow dragons were torn down, and amidst an outburst of cheering the White Ensign was hoisted, closely followed by the red sun of Japan.

My Lieutenant and myself were standing in the square cheering our flag going up, with our men taking cover in a passage, when two Chinese nipped out of a gateway about twenty yards away, and came for us with fixed bayonets, firing their magazines as they marched, from the hip. My Lieutenant had emptied his revolver and was drawing his sword to defend himself when I chipped in and "bagged the brace" '.

[1]This account by Rear Admiral Bruce is generally accepted. However German accounts (*Militär Wochenblatt*) say Commander Pohl was 'one of the first'. Dobrovolski said he heard afterwards that Russians and English led the attack. Stankevitch said 'though the English wavered at first, they finally advanced with the Russians.' Russia claimed that Stankevitch and four of his men were first in but had no flag with them so the British flag was first to be hoisted.

The storming parties then found that the North Fort had been deserted by the garrison, and as they headed for the South Forts the explosion in the main magazine did their work for them. The battle was over. An unexpected amount of opposition was offered by a single 6-inch Q.F. Armstrong in the South Fort, but the captured guns in the last position, in conjunction with the gunboats, succeeded in silencing it after a desperate duel. The gunshield was found to have been struck seven times, and the cement emplacement was literally torn to pieces by shell fire. If the other guns had been served with the same devotion . . .

First over the parapet of the Fort had been the Japanese Commander Hattori, who turning to assist Commander Cradock over the wall was shot dead. A British seaman also fell dead at this point, Ordinary Seaman O.N. 188203 William Theodore Bing of HMS *Barfleur*. Commander Cradock reported that, as well, six men of the British force were wounded in the land attack. It is difficult to ascertain the casualties of the other land forces. Commander Cradock wrote: 'The Foreign forces on shore had also, I am sorry to say, some casualties, including amongst the killed the Japanese commander'. The overall figure for the battle is generally given as 172 killed and wounded. The figures for the ships are better known.

*Algerine*: Mr Herbert J. Hargraves, assistant paymaster-in-charge and 12 men were wounded (though it is not certain whether this figure includes men ashore):
*Gilyak*: 10 men killed, 2 officers and 47 men wounded (most of her casualties were caused by the shell which exploded one of her magazines).
*Iltis*: The gunner and 7 men killed; the captain and 30 men wounded.
*Lion*: One man mortally wounded.
*Koreetz*: 2 officers and several men killed and wounded.
*Bobr*: no casualties.

During the occupation of the Forts both British and German gunners manned captured guns and turned them on the South Forts. There were 450 Chinese found dead in the Fort and it was estimated by a prisoner that a further 50 had been thrown into the moat by their comrades. No-one knows the exact number killed or wounded in the other forts, two of which sustained serious explosions. It is generally thought that the total casualties were around a thousand – a third of the garrison.

Lieut Hans Hellmann of the *Iltis*, killed in action, Taku, June 17.

Commander Wilhelm Lanz wounded before Taku

The list of captured guns in the North West Fort was impressive:

| | | |
|---|---|---|
| 4 × 12 cm | Krupp BL | |
| 4 × 12 pr | smooth bore ML | |
| 8 × 40 pr | rifled ML | |
| 2 × 5 in | Vavaseur BL | |
| 4 × 8 cm | Krupp field-guns BL | |
| 3 × 4 in | brass, rifled ML | |
| 3 × 8 cm | Krupp, iron carriages BL | |
| 4 × 6 pr | Smooth bore, wooden carriages ML | |

Guns bearing on the River:

| | | |
|---|---|---|
| 4 × 12 cm | Krupp BL | |
| 5 × 40 pr | smooth bore ML | |
| 2 × 5 in | Vavaseur BL | |
| 2 × 8 cm | Krupp, on field carriages. | |

Thousands of eyes peered through the gloomy morning at the distant shoreline from the Allied fleet anchored off the Taku Bar. When the firing stopped there was an air of expectancy. Mr Ellis, signal boatswain of HMS *Centurion* watched for flag signals perhaps more carefully than others. He had learned his lesson the hard way. An entry in the ship's log of April 26 that year testified to it: 'Placed Mr Ellis, signal boatswain under arrest, he having neglected his duty by ordering the Russian ensign to be hoisted at the fore whilst a salute from an American ship was being returned'. He had been released from arrest on April 30.

He made no mistake this time, on June 17: 'Observed German gun vessel Iltis coming out of harbour flying Chinese ensign under German at the main. Signalled Forts Taken. 1705. Iltis and Fame came out, cheered ship. 1850. Whiting came out, cheered ship'. China had lost its main chance.

There is always the exception to the rule! This exception is a group of medals to Edwin Goodwin, Chief Stoker with the East and West Africa 'Witu 1890' bar, as a stoker on HMS *Turquoise*: a long service medal awarded while on HMS *Terrible* and the QSA for HMS *Terrible* – then the theoretically impossible combination – China 1900 medal to HMS *Fame* with bar 'Taku Forts'. His service record shows that he actually served on three ships which took part in the China campaign: He joined *Terrible* on 14 September 1899 and left 9 May 1900 for HMS *Barfleur* where he was listed from 10 May to 31 December 1900. Clearly, as he appears on *Fame*'s roll, (his medal was sent to Pembroke 15/10/02 – Roll ADM 171-55) he was lent by *Barfleur* – or may even have taken passage on *Fame* to the China scene from Hong Kong.

# DETAILS OF SOME OF THE OFFICERS INVOLVED

## HMS *Alacrity*

**BROWNE, R.H.J. Staff Surgeon.** Taku Forts and Relief of Pekin bars.
**Royal Navy List 1914:** Surgeon of *Alacrity* during the operations in North China 1900; present at the storming and capture of Taku Forts, mentioned in despatches (China Medal, Taku clasp); present at the relief of Tientsin Settlement, and the subsequent relief of Sir E. Seymour's column at Hsiku (Relief of Pekin clasp) promoted to Staff Surgeon for these services.
**Mentioned in Despatches (Commander Cradock):** 'Surgeon Robley Browne, H.M.S. Alacrity, was quick in his aid and assiduous in his attention to the wounded'.

**CHARRINGTON, E. Lieutenant.** Taku Forts and Relief of Pekin bars.
**Royal Navy List 1914:** Lieutenant of *Philomel*, present on the occasion of the bombardment and capture of the Sultan of Zanzibar's Palace, on 27 August 1896, by the Squadron of Rear-Admiral H.H. Rawson, CB, mentioned in despatches; also served in the punitive naval expedition commanded by Rear-Admiral Rawson, CB and landed from the Squadron to punish the King of Benin for the massacre of the political expedition 1897, ending in the capture of Benin city, 18 February 1897; commanded 7-pounder gun, and rocket tube (General Africa Medal, Benin clasp); present at the capture of Taku Forts, 17 June 1900; served with storming party and was specially mentioned in despatches for gallant conduct; DSO for this service; also present at Relief of Tientsin, Haiku, and capture of Peiyang Arsenal, June 1900 (China Medal 1901).
**Mentioned in Despatches (Commander Cradock):** 'I would especially remark on the fine examples set by Lieutenant Eric Charrington of H.M.S. Alacrity, and . . ., in the firing line, both being worthy of the highest praise'.

**CRADOCK, C.G.F.M. Commander.** Taku Forts and Relief of Pekin bars.
**Royal Navy List 1914:** First Lieutenant of *Dolphin*; served with the Eastern Soudan Field Force as ADC to the Governor General of the Red Sea; present at the battle of Tokar 19 February 1891; and subsequent occupation of Affafit (Khedive's Bronze Star, Tokar clasp, Medjidie of the Fourth Class); mentioned in despatches, was first lieutenant of the sloop *Dolphin* at the rescue by that ship of the entire officers and crew of the Brazilian corvette *Almirante Barroza*, which was totally wrecked under sail on a lee shore on Ros Dil, 1892; author of *Sporting Notes in the Far East* 1890; also *Wrinkles in Seamanship, or a Help to Salt Horse* 1894; Pro. Com. R. Yacht; as commander of *Alacrity*, commanded the British Naval Brigade which led the Allies at the storming and capture of the Taku Forts, 17 June 1900 ('July' incorrectly given in Navy List); noted for promotion for gallantry (China Medal, Taku clasp); commanded British Naval Brigade, and directed the British, American, Japanese, and Italian forces on the advance to and relief of the Tientsin settlement, and again at the subsequent relief of Sir E. Seymour's column at Siku; present with the Naval Brigade

Commander Christopher Cradock RN

at the attack on and capture of the Peiyang Arsenal, Tientsin, 27 June 1900 (Relief of Pekin clasp); awarded by HIM the German Emperor the Royal Order of the Crown, 2nd Class, with swords, for services in China; CB 26 June 1902; MVO April 1903, on the occasion of the visit of HM King Edward VII to Malta; awarded 2nd Class Royal Spanish Order of Naval Merit 1906; has Testimonial of the Royal Humane Society for jumping overboard at night in Palmas Bay, Sardinia, 1904 and saving the life of a drowning midshipman; author of *Whispers from the Fleet*, 1907–1908; aide de camp to the King, 9 February 1909 to 24 August 1910; when he was promoted to rear-admiral; rear-admiral in Atlantic Fleet, August 1911 to August 1912; was at Gibraltar when the P&O's *Delhi* with the Duke and Duchess of Fife and their daughters on board, stranded near Cape Spartel on the night of 12 December 1911; received the Appreciation of their Lords Commissioners of the Admiralty, and on returning to England was received by King George V. and awarded the KCVO (28 February 1912) for Personal Service; also granted the Silver Medal of the Board of Trade for gallantry in saving life on this occasion; Rear-Admiral Commanding Fourth Cruiser Squadron, February 1913.

Rear-Admiral Sir Christopher Cradock was to 'meet his Waterloo' on 1 November 1914, when he commanded the British Squadron at Coronel against von Spee. Outmatched and out-gunned he attempted to disable the German Squadron, flying his flag in HMS *Good Hope*. At 7.00 pm von Spee committed his ships to battle at a range of nearly seven miles. By the third salvo the *Scharnhorst* found Cradock's range. The *Good Hope*'s larger guns were hit and silenced early in the fight – one of them before it had even fired. With the range shortening HMS *Monmouth* was badly hit by *Gneisenau*. *Leipzig* and *Dresden* converged on HMS *Glasgow*. By 7.40 pm HMS *Monmouth* was a mass of flames aft and down by the head. Cradock swung HMS *Good Hope* directly at the Germans. Her midships were ablaze, her main armaments twisted and wrecked but her smaller guns blazing away. Eye-witnesses judged that Cradock was going to try and use his torpedoes. But a well-directed salvo struck HMS *Good Hope* and it blew up. There were no survivors in the icy sea.

There were a number of men who had fought in the China 1900 campaign who went down with the British ships on that occasion, including Ship's Corporal Thomas J. Partridge on HMS *Good Hope*, who had served on HMS *Daphne* in the China War.

On December 8 the British took their revenge and destroyed the German Squadron off the Falklands; HMS *Glasgow* took part in both actions.

**MAY, W. S. Gunner.** Taku Forts and Relief of Pekin.
**Royal Navy List 1914:** Served with the Naval Brigade at the capture of Taku Forts 17 June 1900 and present at the Relief of Tientsin, Kaiku and capture of the Peiyang Arsenal (wounded). (China Medal, Taku and Pekin clasps) highly recommended by Admiral Sir E. H. Seymour; specially promoted 16 March 1905 to chief gunner for services in China.

## HMS *Algerine*

**CHAMBERS, A. S. Lieutenant.** Taku Forts and Relief of Pekin bars.
**Royal Navy List 1914:** Midshipman of *Raleigh*, served in the Naval Brigade landed by Rear-Admiral F. G. D. Bedford, CB, ... at Bathurst on the River Gambia, West Coast of Africa February 1894, in co-operation with the two companies of the 1st West India Regiment for the punishment of Fodi Silah, a rebellious slave-raiding chief (General Africa Medal, Gambia 1894 clasp) Lieutenant of *Algerine*, served at bombardment and capture of Taku Forts 17 June 1900. Slightly wounded, mentioned in despatches. Landed with the Naval Brigade for the Relief of Peking.
**Mentioned in Despatches (Johnston Stewart):** 'Lieutenants Chambers and Duncan were indefatigable in the performance of their duties and in superintending the firing ...'

**COURTIS, E. G. Gunner.** Taku Forts and Relief of Pekin bars.
**Royal Navy List 1914:** Joined Royal Navy 7 December 1888; warrant officer 1 November 1898; served in *Algerine* during Boxer Rebellion in China 1900; during the bombardment of the Taku Forts was gunnery officer of the ship, and succeeded in remounting a 3-pounder quick-firing gun, under fire, in 15 minutes; later, having observed a line of electric observation mines ahead, Mr Courtis went away in a dinghy with one man, and personally performed the dangerous service of destroying five of the enemy's mines by cutting wires, removing detonators and primers, and drowning the mines, thus probably saving many lives; was subsequently landed in charge of two of the ship's 4-inch quick-firing guns, and accompanied them to the Tientsin lines, where they were urgently required to out-range the enemy; took one gun some four miles from the supports and base, and (with the aid of some men of the 1st Chinese Regiment) mounted it on the extreme right flank of the settlement, under a brisk shellfire; remained in command of this gun during the remainder of the bombardment and subsequent capture of Tientsin city; afterwards received a C-in-C's appointment as transport officer at Sin-Ho, which post Mr Courtis held for four months when the *Algerine* left for Hong Kong; chief gunner, 1 November 1913.

**DUNCAN, G. Lieutenant.** Taku Forts and Relief of Pekin bars.
**Royal Navy List 1914:** Lieutenant of *Algerine* in China 1900; present at bombardment of Taku Forts 17 June 1900. Commander Cradock reported on the capture of the Forts: 'Part of the British Force gained an entrance through two gun ports, and over a low part of the ramparts, which were held by my officers through the instrumentality of Lieutenant Duncan, who from previous observations on shore had discovered these weak spots'. Landed in charge of an explosive party under the general command of Lieutenant-Commander Keyes for the destruction of the guns and magazines of Hsin-Cheng Fort. Afterwards engaged in running despatches between Tientsin and the fleet at Taku Bar, and in various transport duties. Three times mentioned in despatches (China Medal).

**HARGREAVES, H. J. Assistant Paymaster.** Single bar Taku Forts.

**REED, J. C. G. Surgeon.** Single bar Taku Forts.
**Royal Navy List 1914:** Surgeon of *Algerine* at taking of Taku Forts 1900 (China Medal with clasp) being on duty at the time in a temporary hospital between the attacking ships and the forts; accompanied the first water party for the relief of Tientsin.

**ROBINSON, S. Lieutenant.** Single bar Taku Forts.
**Royal Navy List 1914:** Lieutenant of *Algerine* at capture of Taku Forts; mentioned in despatches.
**Mentioned in Despatches (Johnston Stewart):** '... while Lieutenant Robinson navigated the ship down river as coolly as if nothing was going on.'

**STEWART, R. H. J. Commander.** Single Bar Taku Forts.
**Royal Navy List 1914:** Commander of the *Algerine* specially promoted for services in connection with the capture of the Taku Forts; of his share in the action Sir E. H. Seymour wrote: 'I would specially mention Commander Johnston Stewart, of H.M. Ship Algerine, the senior naval officer present at Taku (The Rear Admiral being in his flagship outside the bar 12 miles off); Commander Stewart directed our part of the operations, and well and ably handled his ship under heavy fire from the forts in a most gallant seamanlike way, and I desire to submit his name to their Lordships for their very favourable notice.' Their Lordships expressed 'their thorough approbation'. Prussian Royal Crown Order, 2nd Class with Swords 1902; MVO 8 September 1905; rear-admiral 8 September 1909; CB on the Coronation of King George V 19 June 1911.
**Mentioned in Despatches (Rear-Admiral Bruce):** 'I wish to bring most strongly to the notice of their Lordships that the brilliant manner in which Commander Stewart handled his ship, immensely contributed to the success achieved, which at one time was extremely doubtful, and his putting her so close under the Forts that most of their shot went over him, accounts for his small loss.'

**WHITE, A. F. Engineer.** Taku Forts and Relief of Pekin bars.
**Royal Navy List 1914:** Senior engineer of *Blanche* in 1896 employed off coast of Crete during insurrection; engineer in charge of machinery of *Algerine* during bombardment and capture of Taku Forts 17 June 1900; subsequently in charge of repairs to boats employed on transport duties in Pei-ho River and in charge of distilling apparatus at Sinho and Taku during the advance to Pekin; services notes in records at Admiralty. China Medal (Taku Forts and Relief of Pekin clasps).

# HMS *Aurora*

**CRUTCHLEY, A. F. Midshipman.** Taku Forts and Relief of Pekin bars.
**Royal Navy List 1914:** Midshipman of *Aurora* China 1900 (China Medal, Relief of Pekin clasp); served at Tientsin with the Naval Brigade. (List does not mention Taku Forts.)
**KEMP, T. W. Acting Commander.** Taku Forts and Relief of Pekin bars.
**Royal Navy List 1914:** Lieutenant of *Blonde* during the Sierra Leone Rebellion 1898 (General Africa Medal and clasp 1898-9) lieutenant of *Aurora* China 1900. Specially

mentioned for his services in advance on Tientsin; awarded the Order of the Companionship of the Indian Empire for his services whilst in command of *Sphinx* in the Persian Gulf, 1 January 1905; has also received the Mejidie 2nd Class (Turkey) and Order of Commander St. Maurice and St. Lazarus (Italy); qualified interpreter in Hindustani, Arabic and Russian.

**SAMS, C. H. H. Midshipman.** Taku Forts and Relief of Pekin bars.
**Royal Navy List 1914:** Midshipman of *Aurora* China 1900; was one of the party which captured Taku Forts and afterwards served in their garrison until invalided (China Medal, Taku and Pekin clasps).

## HMS *Barfleur*

**ALLEN, H. C. Midshipman.** Taku Forts and Relief of Pekin bars.
**Royal Navy List 1914:** Midshipman of *Barfleur*; mentioned in despatches for services at Tientsin in June 1900.

**CORNABE, W. E. Midshipman.** Taku Forts and Relief of Pekin bars.
**Royal Navy List 1914:** Midshipman *Barfleur*, mentioned in despatches for services at Tientsin in June 1900.

**DIX, C. C. Midshipman.** Taku Forts and Relief of Pekin bars.
**Royal Navy List 1914:** Dix, *C.C.*, midshipman of *Barfleur*; distinguished himself at the attack on the Taku Forts, June 1900, by rescuing a comrade, and disposing of two Chinamen with his revolver; promoted to lieutenant 15 January 1903, for war services in China; lieutenant of *Porpoise* during the operations in Somaliland (General East African Medal, Somaliland 1902-4 clasp); author of *The World's Navies in the Boxer Rebellion*; qualified in Signal Duties 1910-11; flag lieutenant in First Battle Cruiser Squadron, February 1911 to February 1913 and in Third Battle Squadron, July 1913.
**Mentioned in Despatches (Cradock):** '... also the conduct of Midshipman C. Dix, H.M.S. Barfleur, who undoubtedly saved his Lieutenant's life.'

**MAYNE, R. C. Midshipman.** Taku Forts and Relief of Pekin bars.
**Royal Navy List 1914:** Midshipman of *Barfleur* China 1900; mentioned in despatches for services at Tientsin in June 1900; promoted to lieutenant 15 November 1902 for those services.
**Mentioned in Despatches (Keyes):** 'Mr. Mayne, Midshipman of the Barfleur was in command of a guard of seamen with a Maxim, and also did very well.' (He was not in the storming party.)
(Roger Keyes was awarded the Royal Humane Society bronze medal for jumping into the Pei-ho on 8 July 1900 and saving Midshipman R. C. Mayne who was accidentally swept overboard by a rope.)

**SHORE, L. H. Midshipman.** Taku Forts and Relief of Pekin bars.
**Royal Navy List 1914:** Midshipman of *Barfleur* China 1900; mentioned in despatches for his services as ADC to Commander Cradock.
**Mentioned in Despatches (Cradock):** 'I would also respectfully bring before your notice

the pluck and ability of my two ADC's Midshipman . . . and Midshipman Lionel Shore, H.M.S. Barfleur, also . . .'
(Ship's log refers to storming party being landed 'Lieutenant Williams, four Midshipmen . . .')

**TICHBORNE, G. M. Reverend.** Taku Forts and Relief of Pekin bars.
**Royal Navy List 1914:** Chaplain of *Barfleur*, served with Naval Brigade at taking of Taku Forts and also at the relief of Pekin (China Medal two clasps).

**WILLIAMS, R. S. Lieutenant.** Single bar Taku Forts.
**Ship's Log:** 'Landed Lieutenant Williams' 16.6.1900 'for storming party'.

**WROTTESLEY, F. R. Flag Lieutenant.** Taku Forts and Relief of Pekin bars.
**Royal Navy List 1914:** Flag lieutenant of *Barfleur* during operations in North China in 1900; present at taking of Taku Forts (China Medal, Taku Forts and Pekin); received the Royal Order of the Crown of Prussia, 3rd Class, with Swords; lieutenant and first lieutenant of *Victoria and Albert* 1907 to 1909. Pro. Com. R. Yacht 31 August 1909.

## HMS *Centurion*

**KILPATRICK, R. Asst. Engineer.** Taku Forts and Relief of Pekin.
***Battles of the Nineteenth Century*** **(Cassell):** 'At nine o'clock p.m. on the 16th the armoured search-light train was sent off on a reconnaissance towards Tientsin, manned by 100 British, French and German bluejackets, a Hotchkiss and a Maxim gun, and in charge of Lieutenants R*eilly* and Kirkpatrick.'
**G. A. Henty *With the Allies to Pekin*:** 'At nine o'clock a long searchlight train went out under the command of Lieutenants Kirkpatrick and R*iley*, with the twelve-pounder Hotchkiss, two Maxims and a hundred men – German, British and French. It was stoked by British blue-jackets, and was driven by a German engineer from the Iltis.'

**PRICKETT, C. B. Midshipman.** Taku Forts and Relief of Pekin.
**Royal Navy List 1914:** Midshipman of *Centurion*; mentioned in despatches for services at Tientsin in June 1900; received clasps for Relief of Pekin and Taku Forts; landed with despatches in 1900 at Durban, and received medal and clasps for Relief of Ladysmith and Tugela Heights.

**RILEY, E. W. Assistant Engineer.** (Taku Forts?)
**Royal Navy List 1914:** Mentioned in despatches for services with Naval Brigade China 1900. (See entries under Kilpatrick.)

**WALCOTT, C. C. Sub. Lieutenant.** Taku Forts and Relief of Pekin bars.
**Royal Navy List 1914:** Mentioned in despatches for services at Tientsin June 1900.

## HMS *Endymion*

**BRIGGS, H. G. Midshipman.** Single bar Taku Forts.
**Royal Navy List 1914:** Midshipman of *Endymion* during the Boxer Rebellion in North China and was present at the taking of the Taku Forts on 17 June remaining in the Forts for

three months (medal) and Taku Forts clasp.

**HULBERT, A. R. Lieutenant.** Taku Forts and Relief of Pekin bars.
**Mentioned in Despatches (Cradock):** 'I would especially remark on the fine examples set by Lieut ... and Lieutenant R. Hulbert of H.M.S. Endymion, in the firing line, both being worthy of the highest praise.' (Promoted to the rank of commander for this service.) (Ship's log for 16.6.1900: 'Employed equipping and telling off landing party to assist in attacking Taku Forts. 1500. Sent landing party of 31 men and Midshipman Briggs under the command of Lieutenant A. R. Hulbert to Flagship.')

## HMS *Fame*

**KEYES, R. J. B. Lieutenant and Commander.** Taku Forts and Relief of Pekin bars.
**Royal Navy List 1914:** Midshipman of *Turquoise*; served in the Naval Brigade under the command of Vice-Admiral The Hon Sir E. R. Fremantle, KCB Commander-in-Chief East Indies for the punitive expedition against the Sultan of Witu, in East Africa October 1890 (General Africa Medal, Witu 1890 clasp) commander of *Barfleur*, Bronze Medal of Royal Humane Society 8 July 1900 for jumping into the Pei-ho River, China, and saving Midshipman R. C. Mayne of *Barfleur*, who was accidentally swept overboard by a rope; lieutenant and commander of TBD *Fame* in China 1900, did good service, especially in cutting out four Chinese destroyers; received from the Admiralty 'the expression of their Lordships' thorough approbation'; mentioned in despatches by General Gaselee 17 January 1901; promoted commander for these services 9 November 1900. MVO 24 April 1906; received the Italian Order of the Crown (3rd Class) 1906; received the Order of the Iron Crown from the Emperor of Austria on the termination of his appointment as Naval Attaché to His Britannic Majesty's Embassy at Vienna; received the Order of St. Maurice and St. Lazarus from HM the King of Italy on the termination of his appointment as Naval Attaché at Rome 1908; and Redeemer, 3rd Class, Greece 1909; inspecting captain of submarines 14 November 1910 and commodore (S) in charge of Submarine Service 31 August 1912; CB on the Coronation of King George V 19 June 1911.
(Roger Keyes was to be admiral of the fleet.)
**Lords Commissioners of the Admiralty to Commander in Chief, China Station:**
'... to Lieutenants and Commanders Keyes and Colin Mackenzie, who did good service in the 'Fame' and 'Whiting' respectively, especially in their smart cutting out of four Chinese destroyers, and to the other officers and men engaged, an expression of their thorough approbation of the gallantry displayed by them during these successful operations ...'

**MASCULL, G. Gunner.** Single bar Taku Forts.
**Royal Navy List 1914:** Gunner of *Fame* was invested by King Edward with the Conspicuous Service Cross on 16 August 1902 for his gallant conduct during the action with the Taku Forts and the cutting out of the Chinese destroyers on the early morning of the 19 (*sic*) June 1900. He was one of the first of the boarding party which took the Hai Loong, taking a very prominent part in the hand to hand scuffle with her crew, and promptly turning her guns on to a large body of the enemy, sniping from the dockyard walls, and covering a sortie to disperse them. He subsequently took charge of three of the prizes for three days with a very reduced crew. It was impossible to anchor them, their cables having been cut, so it was

necessary to berth them alongside the wharf at Tong-ku, making this a very responsible and anxious duty, owing to the continual sniping and raids from marauding bands from the surrounding houses. He also took part in the surprise and capture of the Hsiu Cheng Fort, rendering most useful assistance in the destruction of guns and magazines; promoted to lieutenant 4 April 1911.

**TOMKINSON, W. Lieutenant.** Taku Forts and Relief of Pekin bars.
**Mentioned in Despatches (Roger Keyes):** '. . . I can only say he did most excellently, as did Lieutenant Tomkinson in charge of the whaler boarding party . . .'

**KNIGHT, G. G. Chief Engineer.** Single bar Taku Forts.
**Mentioned in Despatches (Roger Keyes):** 'Mr. Knight, engineer, was of the greatest assistance in charge aft when I was left with a very small crew and no executive officer.'

## HMS *Orlando*

**HERBERT, D. de C. A. Midshipman.** Taku Forts and Relief of Pekin bars.
**Mentioned in despatches (Cradock):** 'I would also respectfully bring before your notice the pluck and ability of my two A.D.C.'s Midshipman Dennis Herbert, HMS Orlando and . . .'

**HIGGINS, C. Gunner.** Single bar Taku Forts.

**HYDE, R. Lieutenant.**
**Royal Navy List 1914:** Sub lieutenant of *Magpie*; served in the Naval Brigade landed by Rear-Admiral F. G. D. Bedford, CB from the *Raleigh*, *Alecto*, *Magpie*, *Satellite* and *Widgeon* at Bathurst, on the River Gambia, West Coast of Africa in February 1894 in co-operation with two companies of the 1st West India Regiment for the punishment of Fodi Silah, a rebellious slave-raiding chief (General Africa Medal, Gambia 1894 clasp); at capture of the Taku Forts and served with the storming party (China Medal, Taku clasp); lieutenant of *Orlando*; Royal Humane Society's Testimonial on Vellum, 29 June 1899, for attempting to rescue a petty officer of the ship in the Muda River, Penang, river infested with crocodiles.

**PARTINGTON, T. W. E. Midshipman.** Single bar Taku Forts.

**PERFECT, H. M. Lieutenant.** Taku Forts and Relief of Pekin bars.
**Royal Navy List 1914:** In command of *Orlando*'s Naval Brigade during the siege and operations round Tientsin, May to end of July 1900. In command of armoured train at the capture of Taku Forts; at the taking of Tientsin; relief of Admiral Sir E. Seymour's column at Hsiku Arsenal (China Medal, Relief of Pekin and Taku Forts clasps).

**PHILLIPS, H. Boatswain.** Taku Forts and Relief of Pekin bars.

## HMS *Whiting*

**MACKENZIE, C.** Taku Forts single bar.
**Royal Navy List 1914:** 'was in command of TBD Whiting at the bombardment of Taku Forts in June 1900 and did good service, especially in the smart cutting out of four Chinese

destroyers; received from the Admiralty an expression of their Lordships' thorough approbation; D.S.O. for these services November 1900.'

**MORETON, J.A.** Taku Forts single bar.
**Mentioned in Despatches (Mackenzie):** 'I beg to recommend to your notice Lieutenant Moreton of this ship (Whiting), who carried out the operation of boarding the first destroyer in a very able manner.'

Lieut Mackenzie

The two bar list and introduction kindly supplied by Captain K. Douglas-Morris RN

## ROLL FOR NAVAL RECIPIENTS OF THE TWO BARS
## TAKU FORTS — RELIEF OF PEKIN

The roll contains the official number of each recipient, which should assist collectors bent upon further research. Medals earned but not awarded have been omitted. Many readers will know that the letters DD stand for 'Discharged Dead'. The notation of (D) stands for the distribution of a duplicate medal, followed by the year it was issued. In some cases the bars were not sent together, and some were very late awards—notes on these cases are stated beneath the recipient.

The roll contains some well known names, the most illustrious of which must surely be Lieutenant R. J. B. Keyes of *Fame* (later to become Admiral of the Fleet, Lord Keyes of Zebrugge and Dover, GCB, KCVO, CMG, DSO). I commend his biography—*Roger Keyes* by C. Aspinall-Oglander (Hogarth, 1951)—sometimes available in certain bookshops. This book not only covers his dare-devil exploits, and especially his impudent raid and capture of the Hsi-Cheng Fort, but also a good account of the whole affray. The name of Cradock of *Alacrity*, unrecognised at the time as the man in charge of the British contingent in the International Relief Force, along with Russians and Germans, became known when he lost his life as the naval commander in defeat at the battle off Coronel against von Spee's squadron. Lieutenant Tomkinson of *Fame* was, as a vice-admiral, to reap only tares in the Invergordon Mutiny saga.

Rewards for services in China were bestowed upon a few in this roll, amongst whom were Lieutenant Charrington of *Alacrity* who received the DSO, and three lieutenants, Hulbert of *Endymion*, Kemp of *Aurora*, and Keyes of *Fame*, all of whom were simultaneously promoted to the rank of commander.

## ROYAL PRESENTATION OF MEDALS

The notation of (K) against men in this medal roll indicates that the man received his campaign medal from King Edward VII.

By a fortunate coincidence, the campaign medals for the China Incident became available for distribution just prior to the King proceeding upon a west country tour, with its primary aim of laying the foundation stone of the Naval College at Dartmouth.

On the following dull day, 8 March 1902, an impressive and rare event was staged at the Royal Naval Barracks, Devonport, where some 280 China Medals were presented to individuals by the King's own hand; this ceremony being before the Queen, most of the Board of Admiralty, many dignitaries and 3,500 Bluejackets and Marines.

Many 'No Bar', as well as one and two bar medals were royally presented, and it is certain that a number of collectors are unaware that they possess such prestigious medals. The notation can be found in the China 1900 Medal roll at the P.R.O., and there is a complete list of recipients in the *Naval and Military Record* which reported the spectacle.

## HMS *Alacrity*

| | | |
|---|---|---|
| | Browne, R. H. J. | Staff Surgeon,(K) |
| | Charrington, E. | Lieut. |
| | Cradock, C.G.F.M. | Commander (K) |
| 190727 | May, W. S. | Gunner |
| 186195 | Bailey, W. J. | A.B. |
| PO 1970 | Bailey, W. R. | A.B. |
| PLY 7990 | Barr, Jas. | Pte. |
| 355053 | Bertie, John | Pte. |
| 171381 | Bland, H. F. | Dom. 2nd class |
| 290132 | Burgess, G. F. | A.B. |
| PO 5451 | Burrows, Geo. | Stoker |
| 281931 | Clarke, Geo. | Pte. (D) 1907 & 1909 |
| 140261 | Clarke, G. A. | Stoker |
| 178738 | Cliff, W. J. | Chief Stoker |
| 186983 | Corbon, G. W. M. | A.B. |
| 137998 | Dann, G. J. | A.B. |
| 125418 | Frogley, H. T. | P.O. 1st Class |
| 155619 | Griffiths, W. G. | Act. Chief Stoker |
| 183431 | Hayward, G. J. | Ldg. Seaman (D) 1921 |
| 143707 | Hillier, E. J. | A.B. |
| 180904 | Howe, F. | Stoker |
| 279962 | Jehan, H. D. | P.O. 2nd Class |
| 158751 | Lea, H. | Stoker |
| 159215 | Leggett, Geo. | Stoker |
| 186723 | Lockley, J. G. | A.B. |
| 281951 | Longland, R. C. | Stoker |
| 171144 | McKenzie, Geo. | A.B. |
| 284317 | Mitchell, P. H. | Stoker |
| 128984 | Morgan, Thos. | P.O. 1st Class |
| 190791 | Payne, H. W. | A.B. |
| 147447 | Peacock, W. | P.O. 1st Class |
| PO 2753 | Randall, H. Y. | Pte. |
| 151259 | Rendle, Wm. | 2nd Yeo. Sig. |
| PLY 7989 | Robb, T. J. | Pte. |
| 155528 | Robinson, Edw. | P.O. 1st Class |
| 179804 | Shutler, Isaac V. | A.B. |
| 192465 | Stevenson, A. R. | A.B. |
| 183122 | Stratford, J. S. | A.B. |
| 169987 | Tilbury, L. | A.B. |
| 341103 | Townsend, W. J. | A.B. |
| | Wingate, P. C. T. | 3rd Wtr. |

| 192466 | Witts, T. G. | Ord. (D) 1906 |

## HMS *Algerine*

| | | |
|---|---|---|
| | Chambers, A. S. | Lieut. |
| | Courtis, E. G. | Gunner |
| | Duncan, G. | Lieut. |
| | (Sent T. F. bar Feb. 1903, R. of P. bar June 1903. Also both bars 8th October 1903) | |
| | White, A. F. | Engineer |
| | (Sent T. F. bar Feb. 1903, R. of P. bar Oct. 1905) | |
| 160843 | Cackett, J. W. | A.B. |
| 176788 | Godfrey, Frank | A.B. |
| 168115 | Knight, Syd. | A.B. |
| 174705 | Rogers, W. G. | A.B. |
| 193132 | Speare, W. T. | A.B. |

## HMS *Aurora*

| | | |
|---|---|---|
| | Crutchley A. F. | Mid. |
| | Kemp, T. W. | Act. Commander |
| | (Medal presented at Admiralty 24th January 1905) | |
| | Sams, C. H. H. | Mid. |
| 192538 | Baker, P. J. | Ord. |
| 340760 | Barnes, A. J. | Bandsman |
| 142827 | Bowden, R. P. | A.B. |
| 287233 | Brady, J. | Stoker (D) 1917 |
| 185449 | Briggs, A. E. | Ord. |
| 287144 | Burry, F. J. | Stoker |
| 191762 | Callaghan, H. T. | A.B. (D) 1917 |
| 197796 | Catlin, E. J. | Ord. |
| 278171 | Collins, A. | Stoker |
| 192595 | Cosway, W. | Ord. |
| 291729 | Crowley, F | Ord. |
| 194521 | Discombe, F. | Ord. |
| 278241 | Edwards, C. | Stoker |
| 278215 | Finegan, J. | Stoker |
| 192594 | Foale, P. | Ord. |
| 340446 | Franks, A. A. | Bandsman |
| 192570 | German, H. | Ord. |
| 341843 | Gibson, H. | Arm. Cr. |
| 185610 | Ham, G. F. | Ord. |
| 196234 | Heard, A. | Ord. |

| Number | Name | Rank/Rate |
|---|---|---|
| 192587 | Helson, S. J. | Ord. |
| 143508 | Hoare, F. | A.B. |
| 185202 | Hobbs, R. | Ord. |
| 90659 | Horsham, W. | P.O. 1st Class |
| 182749 | Hurcum, H. | Ord. |
| PLY 8797 | Keen, T. | Pte. |
| 287194 | Kennard, W. J. | Stoker |
| 341894 | King, F. | Blacksmith's Mate |
| 190518 | Lang, S. | A.B. |
| 192240 | Martin, A. H. | Ord. |
| 189096 | Moss, C. R. | Ord. |
| 124493 | Parsons, C. W. | Band Corporal |
| 145179 | Paul, J. J. | Chief Yeo. Sig. |
| | (R. of P. bar sent April 1902, T. F. bar Sept. 1904) | |
| 180697 | Roderick, E. E. J. | Ldg. Sig. |
| 193276 | Rowe, J. | Ord. (D) 1904 |
| 191790 | Sharland, T. | Ord. |
| 287154 | Sharp, H. | Stoker |
| 151609 | Smyth, W. J. | A.B. |
| 278528 | Spillane, Jas. | Stoker DD. |
| 111305 | Sullivan, J. | P.O. 1st Class |
| 179183 | Uren, G. | A.B. |
| 129198 | Wells, W. | Bandsman |
| 109114 | Williams, H. E. | A.B. |

## HMS *Barfleur*

| Number | Name | Rank/Rate |
|---|---|---|
| | Allen, H. C. | Mid. |
| | Cornabe, W. E. | Mid. |
| | Dix, C. P. | Mid. (K) |
| | Mayne, R. C. | Mid. |
| | Shore, L. H. | Reverend (K) |
| | Tichborne, G. M. | Flag Lieut. (K) |
| | Wrottesley, F. R. | Stoker |
| 284918 | Abel, H. F. | A.B. |
| 193435 | Astell, H. T. | Pte. |
| CHA. 7352 | Bailey, A. E. | A.B. |
| 188942 | Ball, A. A. | P.O. 1st Class DD. |
| 115738 | Beckingham, V. J. | Ord. |
| 187012 | Blackburn, F. | Gunner |
| RMA. 4206 | Blackman, A. | A.B. |
| 178526 | Blowers, J. G. | |
| 121532 | Brett, S. | P.O. 1st Class |
| 187333 | Brown, J. | A.B. DD. |
| 163183 | Caley, H. E. | P.O. 1st Class (D) 1912 (K) |
| RMA. 6509 | Carter, C. | Gunner |
| 189200 | Carter, J. | A.B. |
| CHA. 3657 | Cassells, C. N. D. | Pte. |
| CHA. 2017 | Clancy, J. | Pte. |
| RMA. 4961 | Cobb, E. W. | Gunner (K) |
| 183066 | Collier, R. K. | A.B. |
| 188389 | Cornish, H. J. | A.B. |
| RMA. 4859 | Crapnell, J. | Gunner |
| 174723 | Downes, J. | Pte. |
| | (R. of P. bar sent June 1902, T. F. bar Jan. 1904) | |
| RMA. 3938 | Dumbrell, J. | Gunner (D) not sent |
| 187300 | Farquharson, F. | A.B. |
| CHA. 8813 | Farthing, C. A. | Lance Corp. |
| 149938 | Field, G. H. | A.B. |
| CHA. 8793 | Green, A. E. | Pte. |
| 188808 | Groves, E. W. | Ord. DD. |
| CHA 6142 | Harrington, H. | Pte. |
| 286335 | Harvey, F. J. | Stoker (D) 1912 |
| 174152 | Higgs, H. E. | Ldg. Seaman |
| CHA. 7464 | Huntley, A. | A.B. |
| 189210 | Hurdle, A. W. | A.B. |
| 164787 | Johnson, F. | A.B. |
| 187299 | Jupp, H. C. | Pte. (D) 1937 |
| CHA. 9179 | Kesbey, J. E. | A.B. DD. |
| 162904 | King, J. | Pte. |
| CHA. 5823 | Lanagan, D. | Gunner |
| PO 8521 | Leach, W. | A.B. |
| RMA. 4851 | Lee, T. J. | Gunner |
| 193153 | Maclaren, H. J. | A.B. |
| RMA. 4861 | Martin, W. J. | Act. Q.M. Sgt. (K) |
| RMA. 3487 | Messenbird, G. H. | Pte. |
| PLY 7513 | Packwood, E. | Pte. |
| CHA. 5667 | Pankhurst, W. | Pte. |
| 181553 | Parsons, E. J. | A.B. |
| 160296 | Price, C. T. | A.B. |
| 187276 | Rubbins, T. | A.B. |
| PO 8261 | Ryman, C. W. | Bugler |
| CHA. 8760 | Shipley, E. | Pte. |
| 187215 | Strudwick, A. | Ord. |

| | | |
|---|---|---|
| CHA. 7264 | Surman, C. | Pte. |
| 189202 | Thake, J. W. | Ord. |
| 187758 | Timmins, W. | A.B. (D) 1915 |
| CHA. 6873 | Tristram, H. J. | Pte. (K) |
| 160237 | Walker, G. W. | Ldg. Seaman |
| 173653 | Walmsley, W. | A.B. |
| CHA. 8772 | Warren, C. | Pte. |
| 171011 | West, C. H. | A.B. |
| 280915 | West, W. J. | Stoker |
| 173149 | Winser, E. | P.O. 2nd Class (D) 1909 |
| 188903 | Wise, H. | A.B. |
| 113195 | Woodward, F. R. | P.O. 1st Class |

## HMS *Centurion*

| | | |
|---|---|---|
| 341474 | Kilpatrick, R. | Asst. Engineer |
| 268184 | Prickett, C. B. | Mid. |
| 281432 | Walcott, C. C. | Act. Lieut. (D) 1927 |
| 114858 | Brown, G. J. | Pntr. 2nd Class |
| CHA. 6151 | Duckworth, F. | E.R.A. 3rd Class (K) |
| 135000 | Evans, E. T. | Stoker |
| 269531 | Fazey, C. | Ldg. Seaman (D) |
| 165126 | Goodwin, S. J. | Pte. |
| 176333 | Hailwood, J. | Ldg. Seaman |
| 163678 | Highbee, E. W. | Act. E.R.A. 4th Class |
| PO 8233 | Hill, S. W. | P.O. 1st Class (K) |
| 182753 | Huffer, H. | A.B. |
| 278052 | Langmaid, W. | Ldg. Shipwright |
| 350119 | Lepla, L. | Pte. |
| 137695 | Lynch, W. G. | A.B. |
| 81108 | Noble, A. | Coopers Crew, DD. |
| 279750 | Parry, F. G. | Ship's Cpl. 1st Class |
| | Perkins, A. J. | A.B. |
| | Tickell, J. C. | Chief Petty Officer |
| | Wilkins, C. | Stoker |

## HMS *Endymion*

| | | |
|---|---|---|
| 289650 | Hulbert, A. R. | Lieut. (K) |
| 167834 | Baines, W. R. | Stoker |
| 287577 | Brett, I. J. | P.O. 1st Class |
| 139352 | Christie, J. | Stoker |
| | Collins, W. | P.O. 2nd Class |

| | | |
|---|---|---|
| 162268 | Crossland, E. | A.B. |
| 158466 | Dennett, J. W. | P.O. 1st Class |
| 145549 | Dering, N. R. | A.B. |
| 171121 | Filmore, J. | A.B. |
| 286119 | Fletcher, F. C. | Stoker |
| 177709 | Hart, M. S. | A.B. |
| 95266 | Hayes, T. | P.O. 1st Class |
| 129029 | Heritage, H. | Chief Stoker |
| 289637 | Hudson, J. W. | Stoker (D) 1906 |
| 289466 | Jacka, W. E. | Stoker |
| 169252 | Jackson, W. A. | Stoker |
| 187481 | Jacob, F. W. | A.B. |
| 110627 | Jeffery, R. | P.O. 1st Class |
| 158209 | Miller, F. D. | Ldg. Seaman (D) 1920 |
| 166138 | Mills, W. | P.O. 2nd Class |
| 155151 | Ransom, J. G. | P.O. 1st Class |
| 144231 | Savage, G. J. | A.B. |
| 108429 | Slater, J. | A.B. |
| 343356 | Swanston, J. | 3rd Wtr. |
| 149337 | Wiltshire, W. J. W. | Ship's Cpl. 1st Class |

## HMS *Fame*

| | | |
|---|---|---|
| | Keyes, R. J. B. | Lieut. Cmdg. (K) |
| | Tomkinson, W. | Lieut. |
| | (T. F. bar June 1902. New Set T. F. & R. of P. Oct. 1902) | |
| 188620 | Brady, H. W. | A.B. |
| | (T. F. bar Feb. 1903. R. of P. bar Nov. 1908) | |

## HMS *Orlando*

| | | |
|---|---|---|
| | Herbert, D. De C. A. | Mid. |
| | Perfect, H. M. | Lieut. |
| | Phillips, H. | Boatswain |
| 128827 | Andrews, J. | A.B. (D) |
| 353478 | Arnold, P. | Arm. Mate |
| 190943 | Batten, W. | A.B. |
| 193704 | Beard, E. E. | A.B. |
| 187880 | Bennett, E. H. | Pte. |
| PO 9127 | Bliss, E. E. V. | A.B. |
| 190471 | Bonner, W. G. | A.B. |
| 151913 | Brown, A. J. | Ldg. Seaman |
| 193990 | Campbell, H. | A.B. |

78

| | | | | | | |
|---|---|---|---|---|---|---|
| 187899 | Coles, H. | A.B. | | 194551 | Murray, N. | A.B. |
| 288538 | Crockford, A. J. | Stoker | | PO 9345 | Mustion, H. T. | Pte. |
| 192439 | Daglish, T. R. | A.B. | | 186703 | Nobbs, W. H. | A.B. |
| 190379 | Davey, F. | A.B. | | 151644 | Olding, P. H. | P.O. 2nd Class |
| 288743 | Davidson, W. | Stoker | | 192171 | Oliver, H. H. | A.B. |
| 144785 | Davis, E. D. | Stoker | | 192956 | Pigott, A. L. | A.B. |
| 287755 | Davis, E. R. W. | Stoker | | 194687 | Planten, T. G. | Ord. |
| 160680 | Doidge, H. | Q.D. Sig. | | PO 3354 | Prows, J. | Pte. |
| 173850 | Dommett, E. G. | A.B. | | PO 7911 | Pulford, H. R. | Pte. |
| 151003 | Dowling, H. C. | Dom. 1st Class | | PO 9237 | Robinson, E. P. | Pte. |
| | (R. of P. bar April 1904. T. F. bar May 1904) | | | 293293 | Robinson, W. | Stoker |
| 191802 | Drury, H. T. G. | A.B. | | 292331 | Roche, J. | Stoker (D) 1907 |
| 187391 | Dunn, W. | A.B. | | 185718 | Rogers, J. E. | A.B. |
| 282213 | Eggleston, G. T. | Stoker | | 194654 | Sidsaff, W. | Ord. |
| 194355 | Elphick, S. | A.B. | | 174174 | Stagg, E. F. | A.B. |
| 279349 | Evans, R. | Ord. | | | (R. of P. bar June 1902. T. F. bar Oct. 1903) | |
| 189622 | Ferris, E. | A.B. | | 147392 | Stripp, A. E. H. | P.O. 2nd Class DD. |
| 187913 | Fletcher, C. | Sig. | | 169625 | Thompson, W. | A.B. |
| 194656 | Fox, A. | A.B. | | 191822 | Thornton, J. | A.B. |
| 154036 | Green, S. J. | A.B. | | 193552 | Toogood, A. | A.B. (D) 1907 |
| 191522 | Grice, E. | A.B. | | PO 2943 | Turner, A. | Pte. |
| 192113 | Hall, J. H. | A.B. | | 287754 | Welch, J. | Stoker |
| 179720 | Hansler, G. A. | Ord. | | 191842 | Whatley, G. | A.B. |
| 188009 | Harris, W. J. | A.B. | | 166197 | White, J. | A.B. |
| 197100 | Holmes, J. N. | A.B. | | 197635 | Wighton, U. | Ord. |
| | (R. of P. bar June 1902. T. F. bar Oct. 1903) | | | 139718 | Wilkinson, H. | Ldg. Seaman |
| 194657 | Howard, J. W. | Ord. | | 197564 | Wood, J. | Ord. |
| 166056 | Joel, W. | Stoker | | 178503 | Wood, S. | A.B. |
| 156990 | Johnson, J. W. | Ldg. Seaman DD | | | | |
| 161921 | Jones, W. T. | A.B. | | | | |
| 283206 | Kimplin, J. J. | Stoker | | | | |
| 162648 | King, G. | Stoker | | | | |
| 126447 | Kipling, J. | P.O. 2nd Class | | | | |
| PO 5991 | Knights, G. | Pte. | | | | |
| 179947 | Lockyer, R. L. | A.B. | | | | |
| 284980 | Mann, G. F. | Stoker | | | | |
| 151373 | Martin, W. T. | Ldg. Seaman | | | | |
| 184357 | Massey, F. T. | A.B. | | | | |
| 191817 | Matthews, G. | A.B. | | | | |
| PO 5211 | May, E. H. | Pte. | | | | |
| 283456 | McDonnell, J. | Stoker | | | | |
| PO 4622 | Murray, J. | Pte. (D) 1913 | | | | |

## HMS *Peacock*

| | | |
|---|---|---|
| PLY 7981 | Veasey, W. | Pte. |

## Abstract of awards to ships

| | |
|---|---|
| HMS *Alacrity* | 42 |
| HMS *Algerine* | 9 |
| HMS *Aurora* | 46 |
| HMS *Barfleur* | 68 |
| HMS *Centurion* | 20 |
| HMS *Endymion* | 25 |
| HMS *Fame* | 3 |
| HMS *Orlando* | 80 |
| HMS *Peacock* | 1 |

## HMS *Alacrity* One bar Taku Forts

| | | |
|---|---|---|
| 152591 | Denham, G. T. | Stoker |
| 169141 | Jordan, J. F. | A.B. |
| 170312 | Keaton, E. J. | Ldg. Seaman |
| 193109 | Moore, R. E. | A.B. |
| 152920 | Macey, A. S. | Arm's Mate |
| 158118 | Worth, John | Stoker |
| 143542 | Wood, A. E. | A.B. |

## HMS *Algerine* One bar Taku Forts

| | | |
|---|---|---|
| 106778 | Adey, W. H. | Ldg. Seaman |
| 342566 | Boland, Wm. | Carpenter's Crew |
| 185926 | Brooks, D. | A.B. (D) |
| 184541 | Brown, F. H. | A.B. |
| 280079 | Browne, J. | Stoker |
| 291752 | Burn, E. C. | Stoker |
| PLY 9443 | Clarke, James | Pte., R.M. (D) |
| – | Chan, O. H. | Dom. 2nd Class |
| 197467 | Claypitt, S. D. | Ord. |
| 121130 | Cook, John | Chief Stoker |
| PLY 3227 | Corber, S. S. | Pte., R.M. |
| 163298 | Couch, A. C. | A.B. |
| 203576 | Crews, W. J. | Ord. |
| 291556 | Crossan, Josh | Stoker (D) |
| 203572 | Curran, Corn's | Ord. |
| 199445 | Darlington, H. | Boy 1st Class |
| PLY 5219 | Davies, James | Pte., R.M. |
| 147138 | Day, W. | P.O. 2nd Class |
| 170694 | Dimon, T. A. | A.B. |
| PLY 5807 | Dimond, F. | Pte., R.M. |
| 280954 | Dodd, W. H. | Stoker |
| 161022 | Dolbear, S. W. | A.B. (D) |
| 154363 | Edgcombe, W. T. | 2nd Yeo. Sig. |
| 115727 | Edwards, Thomas | Sailmaker |
| 142136 | Evans, J. G. | Ldg. Shipwright |
| 127081 | Fry, Samuel | A.B. |
| 197949 | Furnaess, Wm. | Ord. |
| 350403 | Gibson, Wm. | S.B.A. |
| 163825 | Guley, Frederick | A.B. |
| 127090 | Hales, F. L. | P.O 2nd Class |
| – | Hargreaves, H. J. | Asst. Paymaster |
| 118276 | Hemmens, A. | Ship's Cpl. 1st Class |
| 198728 | Hill, A. L. | Ord. |
| 156796 | Hooper, Wm. | A.B. |
| 290886 | Humphreys, E. | Stoker |
| PLY 9441 | Iles, Samuel | Pte., R.M. |
| 119229 | Jarvis, Henry | A.B. |
| 195501 | Jago, Charles | Act. Chief Stoker |
| 138048 | Jay, R. | Dom 2nd Class |
| – | Jay, A. L. | Ldg. Sig. |
| 156432 | Johnson, A. G. | Ldg. Stoker 1st Class |
| 169289 | Johnston, M. | Stoker |
| 283056 | King, Stephen | Chief Stoker |
| 126384 | Knight, G. H. | Lance Corp. |
| PLY 7869 | Lamping, F. | Ldg. Seaman |
| 136368 | Larkworthy, F. | Ldg. Stoker 2nd Class |
| 154927 | Lawrence, J. | Stoker |
| 280670 | Lee, Wm. | Chief Petty Officer |
| 99037 | Lytton, E. | Stoker |
| 279622 | Manning, F. | Chief Carpenter's Mate |
| 140959 | Martin, P. | E.R.A. 3rd Class |
| 268641 | Merryfield J. H. R. | Dom 2nd Class |
| – | Moy, A. L. | A.B. |
| 192370 | Newman, H. | P.O. 1st Class |
| 139164 | Newton, T. | Stoker |
| 165874 | Norman, G. R. | A.B. |
| 145271 | Obrien, D. | Shipwright |
| 173838 | Oliver, J. | Ptnr 2nd Class |
| 342917 | Pascoe, Josh | P.O. 1st Class (D) |
| 342041 | Pateyjohns, J. C. | A.B. |
| 147869 | Perrett, R. F. | Pte., R.M. |
| 145277 | Pinn, C. H. | Stoker |
| PLY 8707 | Phillips, F. | Surgeon |
| 291747 | Pope, J. W. | Lieut., R.N. |
| – | Reed, J. C. G. | Pte., R.M. |
| – | Robinson, S. | A.B. |
| PLY 9444 | Ratel, P. G. | Ldg. Seaman |
| 133666 | Rendle, W. R. | Dom 3rd Class |
| 164759 | Ridge, A. W. | S.P. Steward |
| PLY 5985 | Rose, John | Ldg. Seaman (D) |
| 141680 | San, A. L. | |
| 155829 | Silvester, T. C. | |
| | Smith, C. E. M. | |

| | | |
|---|---|---|
| 186019 | Webb, T. J. | Ord. |
| — | Williams, R. S. | Lt., R.N. |

## HMS *Centurion* One bar Taku Forts

| | | |
|---|---|---|
| PO 8246 | Lee, G. | Pte., R.M. |
| PLY 5167 | McCardle, J. | Cpl. R.M. |
| PO 8255 | O'Neale, E. | Pte., R.M. |
| PO 8277 | Smith, A. J. | Pte., R.M. |
| PO 5611 | Smith, C. H. | Sig. |
| 185837 | Taylor, F. W. H. | Sig. |
| RMA. 5752 | Wales, A. | Gunner |

## HMS *Endymion* One bar Taku Forts

| | | |
|---|---|---|
| — | Briggs, H. G. | Mid. |
| 163394 | Bartlett, E. C. | A.B. |
| 165757 | Chadwick, F. | A.B. |
| 281591 | Evans, J. | Stoker |
| 160933 | Green, W. C. | Ldg. Seaman |
| 160692 | Meerin, W. | A.B. |
| 160886 | Rose, C. | P.O. 2nd Class |
| 171606 | Wyatt, E. J. | A.B. |
| 124719 | Wiley, R. C. | 2nd Yeo. Sig. |

## HMS *Aurora* One bar Taku Forts.

| | | |
|---|---|---|
| 282834 | Ahern, P. | Stoker (D) |
| 192243 | Ainger, F. G. P. | Ord. |
| 191483 | Clarke, J. R. | Ord. |
| 197545 | Clemens, E. | Ord. |
| 183684 | Lamb, G. R. | Ord. (D) |
| 148426 | McCabe, R. | Bandsman |
| 160728 | Philp, T. | Ldg. Stoker 2nd Class |
| 124331 | Powell, G. J. | P.O. 1st Class |
| 110207 | Urell, S. S. | Carpenter's Mate |

## HMS *Fame* One bar Taku Forts

| | | |
|---|---|---|
| 285245 | Aldworth, J. | Stoker |
| 188455 | Bannister, A. | Q.D. Sig. |
| 125845 | Bartlett, G. | Ldg. Stoker 1st Class (D) |
| 292693 | Bickham, W. | Stoker |
| 167786 | Burton, W. | Stoker |

| | | |
|---|---|---|
| 151862 | Smale, A. | Ldg. Stoker 1st Class |
| 191701 | Snowden, A. A. | Sig. |
| 269393 | St. John, E. S. | E.R.A. 4th Class |
| — | Stewart, R. H. J. | Commander |
| 281630 | Sweeny, P. | Stoker |
| 162913 | Thomas, F. | Ldg. Sig. |
| 291748 | Thorne, R. | Stoker |
| 150790 | Tucker, G. H. M. S. | P.O. 1st Class |
| 196284 | Vernon, J. R. G. | Ord. |
| 161442 | Wackley, R. M. | Sgt., R. M. |
| PLY 5091 | Vincent, W. H. F. K. | Arm's Mate |
| — | Why, A. L. | Dom 2nd Class |
| 178938 | Willcox, H. J. | A.B. |
| 190171 | Wiltshire, H. W. | Ord. |
| PLY 9442 | Wise, T. W. | Pte., R.M. |
| 152523 | Wood, G. T. | 2nd Ship's Cook |
| PLY 8842 | Woods, J. F. | Pte., R.M. |
| 203573 | Woolford, W. | Ord. |
| 141579 | Wyatt, C. E. | E.R.A. 2nd Class |
| — | You, A. L. | Dom 3rd Class |

## HMS *Barfleur* One bar Taku Forts (21)

| | | |
|---|---|---|
| CHA. 6173 | Aves, G. | Pte., R.M. |
| 192299 | Barnett, F. C. | A.B. |
| 188072 | Bowers, F. G. | Ord. |
| 179689 | Brackey, H. W. | A.B. |
| 280317 | Brown, T. | Stoker |
| 188203 | Bing, W. J. | Ord. |
| 187196 | Coombes, F. J. | Ord. |
| 157791 | Cullingford, G. E. | 2nd Yeo. Sig. |
| 188400 | Davis, C. F. | A.B. |
| 197636 | Holtley, J. H. | A.B. |
| 123342 | L'aime W. J. | Chief Stoker |
| 185323 | Long, W. T. | A.B. |
| 188076 | Merchant, R. | Naval Instructor |
| 186907 | Midgley, H. W. | A.B. |
| 153195 | Octgenn, J. R. | P.O. 1st Class |
| 125081 | Oliver, T. | Chief Petty Officer |
| 188043 | Parks, A. E. | Ord. |
| 144693 | Pearl, R. | P.O. 2nd Class |
| | Watson, J. W. | |

| | | |
|---|---|---|
| 135737 | Carroll, G. | P.O. 1st Class |
| 140413 | Cassells, F. | Chief Stoker |
| 283131 | Chapman, F. | Stoker |
| 283530 | Conlon, M. | Stoker |
| 284950 | Cook, T. J. | Stoker |
| 269212 | Coppleston, W. J. | Act. E.R.A. 4th Class |
| 299832 | Devlin, H. | Stoker (D) |
| 279555 | Dunstel, W. | Stoker |
| 153932 | Edge, F. P. | Stoker |
| 187226 | Faulkner, E. | A.B. |
| 288142 | Fawcett, J. | Stoker |
| 283626 | Fitch, F. | Stoker |
| 292137 | Fitzpatrick, W. | Stoker |
| 292305 | Furzland, F. J. | Stoker |
| 130321 | Goodwin, E. | Chief Stoker |
| 164151 | Hallifax, C. | Ldg. Stoker 1st Class |
| 186213 | Hannagan, J. | A.B. |
| 282594 | Howard, S. | Stoker |
| 132608 | Jackson, G. | P.O. 2nd Class |
| 174385 | Jeffs, J. | Stoker |
| 282609 | King, H. | Stoker |
| – | Knight, G. G. | Chief Engineer |
| 151884 | Lawson, R. | Stoker |
| 284925 | Lillie, F. H. | Stoker |
| 177224 | Lockett, T. W. | A.B. |
| 187477 | Mace, R. J. | A.B. |
| 154723 | Marshall, J. Y. | Stoker |
| – | Mascull, G. | Gunner |
| 171543 | McKenzie, J. | Ldg. Sig. |
| 187378 | Nye, H. W. | A.B. |
| 281589 | Orsborn, H. | Stoker |
| 268601 | Pamely, A. | E.R.A. 3rd Class |
| 189405 | Parrott, W. | A.B. |
| 138418 | Partridge, A. T. | Stoker |
| 283498 | Pearson, W. | Chief E.R.A. 2nd Class |
| 134471 | Pidgeon, A. J. | Stoker |
| 279734 | Putt, J. | Stoker |
| 283609 | Riddle, E. C. | A.B. |
| 185498 | Royce, W. C. | Act. E.R.A. 4th Class |
| 269310 | Scott, G. L. | Stoker |
| 283496 | Sears, G. T. | Ldg. Stoker 1st Class |
| 161183 | Shapter, J. W. | Ldg. Stoker 1st Class |
| 152238 | Shaw, H. J. | Carpenter's Mate |
| 341108 | Simmonds, W. A. | Dom 2nd Class |
| 284896 | Tack, A. L. | Stoker |
| 186900 | Taylor, F. | A.B. |
| 185988 | Thomas, W. | A.B. |
| 181893 | Tuttle, G. H. | A.B. |
| 283499 | Wanstall, T. W. | Stoker |
| 118656 | Whitehead, H. | Chief Stoker |
| 280355 | Wicks, W. G. | Stoker |
| 282805 | Witty, J. T. | Stoker |
| 187788 | Willey, W. H. | A.B. |
| 147673 | Worthington, J. G. | P.O. 1st Class |
| – | Young, W. J. | |

## HMS *Orlando* One bar Taku Forts

| | | |
|---|---|---|
| 191839 | Ashley, F. | A.B. |
| 198657 | Baker, J. H. | Ord. |
| 199040 | Barnes, A. | Ord. |
| 138734 | Burgess, S. | P.O. 1st Class |
| 194136 | Cuddon, E. G. | Ord. |
| 193365 | Cutler, F. H. | Ord. |
| 181804 | Dale, R. R. | A.B. |
| 287761 | Edmonds, W. | Stoker |
| 191352 | England, F. J. | A.B. |
| 191413 | French, R. | A.B. |
| 138133 | Green, B. | Chief Stoker |
| 193402 | Grier, W. J. | Ord. |
| – | Higgins, C. | Gunner |
| 138929 | Harms, C. | P.O. 1st Class |
| 117007 | Halloran, T. | P.O. 1st Class |
| 139866 | Hamilton, T. E. | Chief Stoker |
| 186123 | Hughes, J. F. | A.B. |
| – | Hyde, R. | Lieut., R.N. |
| 150890 | Lee, J. | P.O. 1st Class |
| 286281 | McDonnell, W. H. | Stoker |
| 184090 | Osborne, S. | A.B. |
| – | Partington, T. W. E. | Mid. |
| 350150 | Painter, E. | Ship's Cpl. 1st Class |
| 197231 | Perkins, D. G. | Ord. |
| 197645 | Peterson, A. | Ord. |
| 196114 | Proctor, F. E. | A.B. |
| 197821 | Sewell, F. A. | A.B. |
| 282996 | Spink, F. | Stoker |
| 158727 | Steel, A. | Ldg. Stoker 1st Class (D) |
| 292322 | Vick, H. J. | Stoker |

| | | |
|---|---|---|
| 194444 | Watson, G. W. | Ord. |
| 187935 | Westbrook, E. E. | A.B. |
| 194341 | White, E. | Ord. |
| 192849 | Whitaker, W. H. | A.B. |
| 132982 | Wood, W. | P.O. 1st Class |
| 190904 | Worth, A. J. | A.B. |

## HMS *Whiting* One bar Taku Forts

| | | |
|---|---|---|
| 269362 | Bates, H. F. | Act. E.R.A. 4th Class |
| 130745 | Butler, H. | Ldg. Stoker 1st Class |
| 292737 | Broom, F. | Stoker |
| 175469 | Cole, W. J. | A.B. |
| 141652 | Carr, W. T. | Chief E.R.A. nd Class |
| 142114 | Cullinane, J. | Act. Chief Stoker |
| 282607 | Cook, W. W. | Stoker |
| 283151 | Deed, J. C. | Stoker |
| 279805 | Doughty, J. | Stoker |
| 117357 | Edwards, W. | P.O. 2nd Class |
| 283145 | Fairman, J. | Stoker (D) |
| 292697 | Ford, T. | Stoker |
| 292722 | Flynn, T. | A.B. |
| 181677 | Giles, T. | A.B. |
| 182459 | Grady, J. | Ldg. Sig. |
| 165308 | Gowen, H. G. | Ldg. Stoker 1st Class |
| 153582 | Gayford, A. | Stoker |
| 282617 | Goff, A. | Stoker (D) |
| 282782 | Greenwood, C. | Stoker |
| 282818 | Grierson, R. | Stoker |
| 282793 | Harris, E. | Stoker |
| 282801 | Hayes, C. | Stoker (D) |
| 283033 | Harding, C. | Stoker |
| 282767 | Jones, J. C. | Stoker |
| 292741 | Jefford, A. E. | A.B. |
| 180252 | Laver, J. G. | Lieut., Commanding |
| – | Mackenzie, C. | Lieut., R.N. |
| 140920 | Moreton, J. A. | Chief Stoker |
| 282807 | McGrath, W. J. | Stoker (D) |
| 280462 | Neal, J. | Stoker |
| 176567 | New, W. | A.B. |
| 190564 | Osbournt, E. A. | Qtr. Dk. Sig. |
| 282754 | O'Norley, T. | Stoker |
| 186998 | Payne, F. | Gunner (W.O.) |
| 166537 | Peat, J. | A.B. |
| 268596 | Painter, F. | A.B. |
| 282798 | Peed, D. | E.R.A. 3rd Class |
| 283130 | Perkins, A. | Stoker |
| 156952 | Pilcher, A. S. | Stoker (D) |
| 340873 | Ritchie, W. H. | A.B. |
| 283149 | Roper, R. | Cook's Mate |
| 290660 | Rushworth, J. | Stoker |
| – | Rowe, T. | Stoker |
| 190333 | Stearn, W. J. | Engineer |
| 282795 | Shovler, E. | A.B. |
| 279612 | Smith, F. | Stoker (D) |
| | Saunders, H. L. | Stoker (D) |
| | Sive, A. L. | Dom. 2nd Class |
| 187274 | Thompson, T. | A.B. |
| 268017 | Thomas, A. | E.R.A. 3rd Class (D) |
| 135421 | Townsend, T. W. W. | P.O. 1st Class |
| 119154 | Warn, R. T. | P.O. 1st Class |
| 141136 | Watson, D. | Chief Stoker |
| 172810 | Wood, R. | Ldg. Stoker 2nd Class |
| 277212 | Walton, A. | Stoker |
| 281299 | Clorain, T. | Stoker RTM 22 |
| 178772 | Neaves, J. H. | A.B. RTM 22 |

D = Duplicate medal issued.
RTM = Medal returned to Mint in 1922.

HMS *Alacrity*

HMS *Aurora*

HMS *Barfleur*

HMS *Centurion*

HMS *Endymion*

HMS *Fame*

HMS *Orlando*

HMS *Whiting*

HMS *Alacrity*

HMS *Whiting*

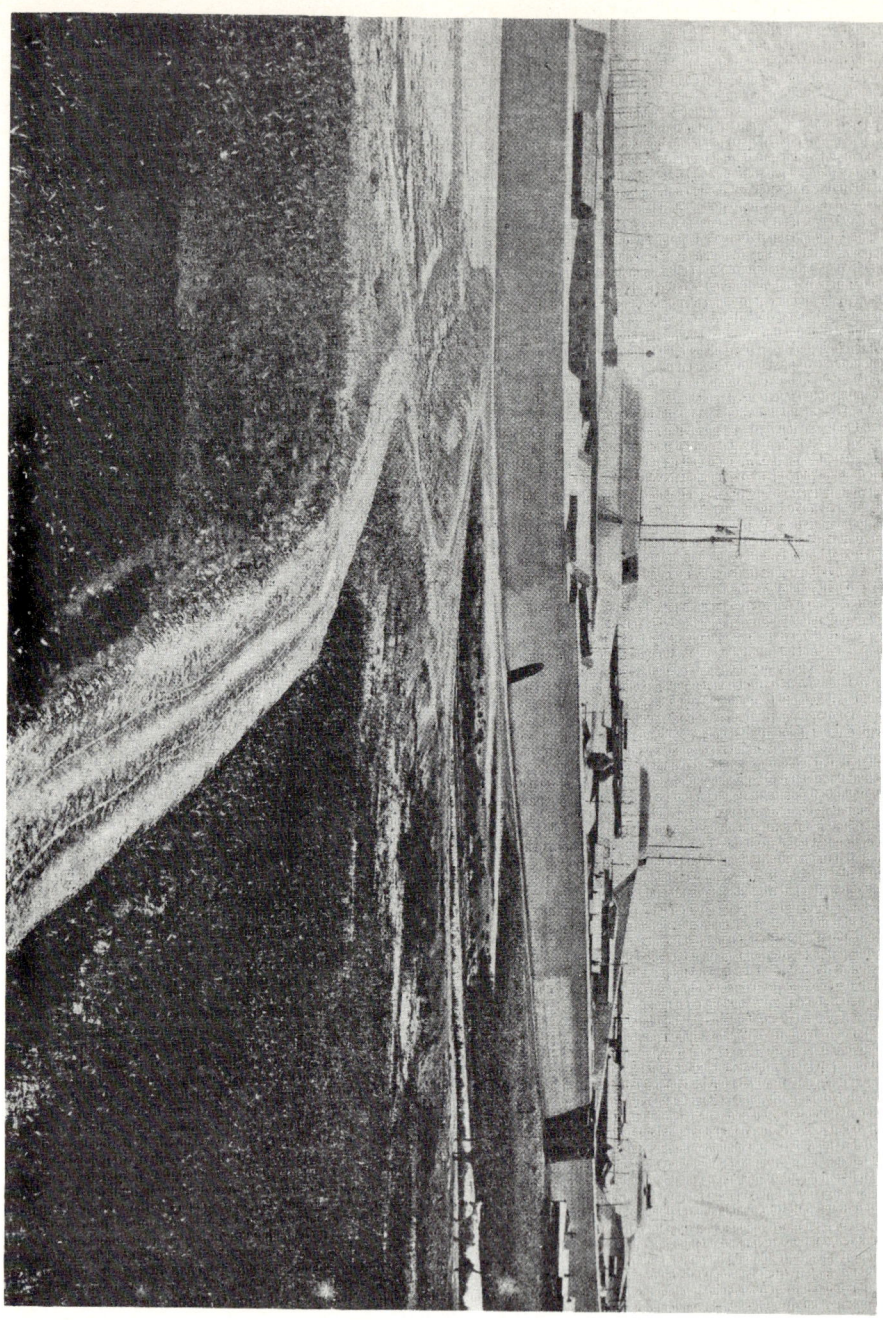

Taku Forts

The powerful guns of the Taku Forts silenced by HM Royal Marines and seamen. A marine stands guard.

## BIBLIOGRAPHY

*The London Gazette*s for October and November 1900.
Gordon's *British Battles and Medals*.
*The Siege of Peking* by Peter Fleming.
*The Royal Navy* by Clowes.
*The Commission of HMS Terrible* by George Crowe, MAA.
*The World's Navies in the Boxer Rebellion* by Lieutenant C.C. Dix RN.
*Destroyer* by Ewart Brookes.
*Fifty-Five Days of Terror* by Burt Hirschfeld.
*With the Allies to Pekin* by G. A. Henty.
*The Story of the Chinese Crisis* by Alexis Krausse.
*The Boxer Rebellion* by Christopher Martin.

Colin Narbeth was born in 1929 at Walton-on-Naze and was educated at Canford, Wimborne, Dorset.

He served for seven years in the Royal Navy, then for 15 years he was a journalist and launched *Stamp Weekly*, a web-offset weekly tabloid newspaper for stamp collectors of which he was Editor for three years.

In 1970 he joined Stanley Gibbons to form a banknote and coin dealing subsidiary, Stanley Gibbons Currency Limited.

A keen collector since he was eight years old, Colin founded the International Banknote Society in 1961 and is the author of many books and articles on collecting subjects.

Colin is 50 years old, married and has three grown-up children.